Zeus Ruler of all, I saved my brothers and sisters after they were swallowed by our dad. *Some family!*

Zeus Sometimes I wish I had just let Dad swallow you all for good!

Hades
I DARE you to come down here and say that, Bro!

Cerberus
WOOF!

Echo
WOOF! WOOF! WOOF! WOOF! WOOF! WOOF! WOOF! WOOF! WOOF! WOOF! ...

Heracles
Here, Cerberus! Wanna play fetch?

Athena
QUIET! I am trying to think!

Pan invites everybody to a party on Mount Olympus tonight @ 8.

 Poseidon
POOL PARTY! Cowabunga, dude!

 Pandora
A party! I'll bring a gift!

 Echo
PARTY! PARTY! PARTY! PARTY! PARTY! PARTY! PARTY! PARTY! PARTY! PARTY! ...

 Aphrodite
Yay! Party! An excuse to get a MANi-pedi!

 Hera
Z, what do you mean "Status: Single"?

CONTENT CONSULTANT
William Hansen
Professor Emeritus of Classical Studies and Folklore
Indiana University, Bloomington

Library of Congress Cataloging-in-Publication Data

Bryant, Megan E.
Oh my gods! : a look-it-up guide to the gods of mythology / Megan E. Bryant.
p. cm. -- (Mythlopedia)
Includes bibliographical references and index.
ISBN-13: 978-1-60631-026-7 (lib. bdg.)   978-1-60631-058-8 (pbk.)
ISBN-10: 1-60631-026-7 (lib. bdg.)   1-60631-058-5 (pbk.)
1. Mythology, Greek--Juvenile literature. I. Title.
BL783.B79 2009
398.2093801--dc22

2009017169

All rights reserved. Published by Franklin Watts, an imprint of Scholastic Inc.
Published simultaneously in Canada. Printed in the United States of America.
SCHOLASTIC, FRANKLIN WATTS, and associated logos are
trademarks and/or registered trademarks of Scholastic Inc.
1 2 3 4 5 6 7 8 9 10 R 18 17 16 15 14 13 12 11 10   23

MYTHLOPEDIA

OH MY GODS!

Where's the party?

A Look-It-Up Guide to the Gods of Mythology

MEGAN E. BRYANT

SCHOLASTIC

OH MY GODS!

*Are you
blowing us kisses?*

PROFILES AND MYTHS
Up close and personal with the gods of the pantheon

The Graces

Speech bubble: *I am a windy god!*

Zephyrus

TMI

THE MYTHLOPEDIA INTRODUCTION

Are you ready to get your myth on? Then you've come to the right place: MYTHLOPEDIA, your one-stop shop for everything you need to know about the stars of Greek mythology. From gods and monsters to goddesses and heroes, the myths that rocked the ancient world are ready to rock yours—if you're ready to read on! But first, check out a little background info that will help you make sense of these amazing characters and stories.

So, what is mythology?

Good Question! "Mythology" is the word used to describe *all* the myths of a particular society. People who specialize in studying myths are called "mythologists." From the Yoruba of West Africa to the Inca of South America, from the Norse of Europe to the Navajo of North America, every culture has its own myths that help us understand its customs and ways of viewing the world.

What is a myth?

Simply put, a "myth" is a kind of story. But not just any old story! Most myths have one or more of these characteristics:

- ➤ Myths are usually about gods or supernatural beings with greater powers and abilities than ordinary humans.

- ➤ Myths explain the origins of the world or how human customs came to be.

- ➤ Myths take place in a time long, long ago, usually in the earliest days of humanity (or just before humans showed up on Earth).

- ➤ Myths were usually thought to be true by their original tellers—no matter how wild or strange they seem to us.

TWO NAMES, POWERS THE SAME

Many gods and goddesses have both Greek and Roman names. That's because the ancient Romans adopted a great deal of Greek mythology and made it their own, often by changing the name of a particular god or goddess. Generally, that deity's powers and myths stayed the same— even though he or she had a new name. As a result, the study of Greek and Roman mythology is often grouped together under the name "classical mythology."

> ## What is the purpose of myths?

A better question might be, What *isn't* the purpose of myths? Myths can:

- explain how things came to be—like the origin of the universe or the creation of humans;
- teach people about the values and beliefs that are important in their society; and
- contain deep religious significance to the people who tell and believe in them.

Perhaps most importantly, studying myths can teach us about people around the world—their cultures and what is (or was) important to them.

> ## Do myths really matter today? After all, mortals have reality TV.

Absolutely! References to Greek mythology are all around us.

- Ever heard of Nike brand athletic gear? Meet Nike, personification and goddess of victory.
- What would Valentine's Day be without the god of love, Cupid, or Eros, as the ancient Greeks called him?
- Does *Apollo 13* ring a bell? The first crewed U.S. space missions were named for Apollo, the god of archery and prophecy.

Bottom line: References to ancient myths are everywhere, from science to pop culture, and knowing about them will help you understand more about the world we live in.

HOW DID WE LEARN THESE STORIES?

At first, Greek mythology was passed along orally through storytelling, songs, and poetry. We learned the stories from written versions, mainly Homer's epic poems *The Iliad* and *The Odyssey*, which tell about the great deeds of heroes. Other sources are Hesiod's *Theogony*, which describes the origins of the world and the gods, and the *Homeric Hymns*, a collection of poems addressed to different gods.

OMG

WHAT'S A TYPICAL DAY LIKE FOR A GOD ON MOUNT OLYMPUS?

In a word: Wild! Without naming names, a certain god turned a nymph into a tree, a grumpy dad swallowed his kids one-by-one, and a winged cherub was accused of fly-by shootings. Sound like a reality show? It's all true!

But these gods were worshipped by mortals for hundreds of years (not anymore—but don't tell them). They were beloved equally for their divine powers and their all-too-human shortcomings. In fact, the Romans adopted them as their own, giving them their more familiar aliases, such as Jupiter for Zeus, Mercury for Hermes, and … Apollo for *Apollo?*

We could go on and on, but the gods can say it so much better themselves. So get ready, mortals. You're about to get up close and personal with some of the biggest, craftiest, and most powerful (shout out to Zeus!) gods of Greek mythology!

Zeus Here's the gods' honest truth ...

OH MY GODS!

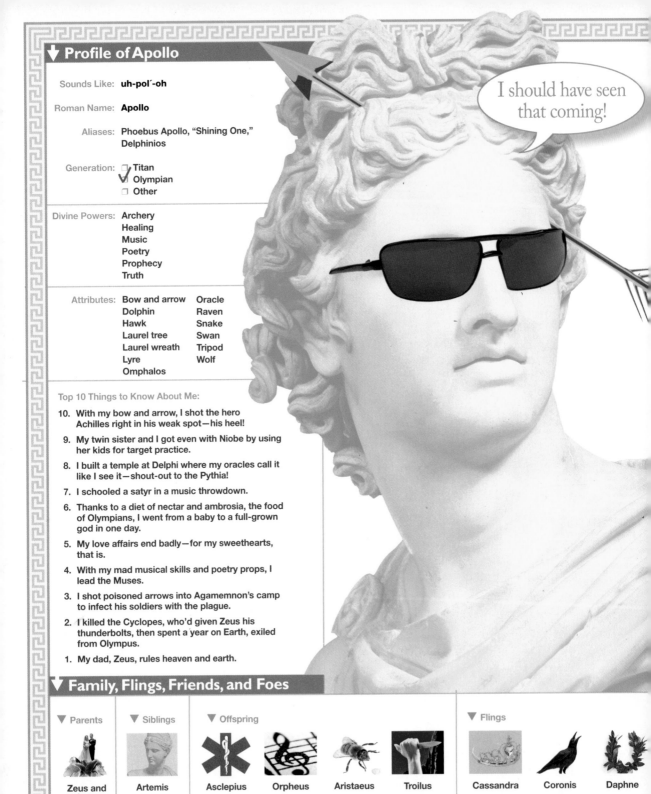

Profile of Apollo

Sounds Like: uh-pol´-oh

Roman Name: Apollo

Aliases: Phoebus Apollo, "Shining One," Delphinios

Generation:
- ☐ Titan
- ☑ Olympian
- ☐ Other

Divine Powers:
Archery
Healing
Music
Poetry
Prophecy
Truth

Attributes:
Bow and arrow · Oracle
Dolphin · Raven
Hawk · Snake
Laurel tree · Swan
Laurel wreath · Tripod
Lyre · Wolf
Omphalos

I should have seen that coming!

Top 10 Things to Know About Me:

10. With my bow and arrow, I shot the hero Achilles right in his weak spot—his heel!

9. My twin sister and I got even with Niobe by using her kids for target practice.

8. I built a temple at Delphi where my oracles call it like I see it—shout-out to the Pythia!

7. I schooled a satyr in a music throwdown.

6. Thanks to a diet of nectar and ambrosia, the food of Olympians, I went from a baby to a full-grown god in one day.

5. My love affairs end badly—for my sweethearts, that is.

4. With my mad musical skills and poetry props, I lead the Muses.

3. I shot poisoned arrows into Agamemnon's camp to infect his soldiers with the plague.

2. I killed the Cyclopes, who'd given Zeus his thunderbolts, then spent a year on Earth, exiled from Olympus.

1. My dad, Zeus, rules heaven and earth.

Family, Flings, Friends, and Foes

▼ Parents
Zeus and Leto

▼ Siblings
Artemis

▼ Offspring
Asclepius · Orpheus · Aristaeus · Troilus

▼ Flings
Cassandra · Coronis · Daphne

APOLLO
LONELY ON MOUNT OLYMPUS

Handsome god of prophecy, archery, music, and more seeks a special someone who won't "make like a tree and leave" when she sees me. I have many talents and can see into the future. Well, except when it comes to love. If you like hawks, music, and poetry, and are ready to be treated like a goddess, shoot me an arrow with your number attached. Laurel trees, no need to apply!

Heads up, handsome!

REALITY CHECK

In the 1960s, NASA named its crewed space program Apollo, after the god of archery and prophecy.

Want to know more? Go to: www.nasm.si.edu/collections/imagery/apollo/apollo.htm

Eros

▼ Friends

The Pythia

Poseidon

Dionysus

▼ Foes

Hera

Python

Eros

Agamemnon

Niobe

Marsyas

APOLLO

"The future's so bright, I gotta wear shades."

MYTH LOPEDIA

Απλλων

IT'S GREEK TO ME

Personification, or giving human characteristics to a nonhuman thing, is BIG in Greek mythology. For example, the little island of Delos worried that after Apollo was born, he would be ashamed of the modest island. Leto, Apollo's mom, vowed to build a temple there and Delos happily agreed to be the god's birthplace.

"From the moment I was born, I always had nectar and ambrosia in my crib."

Chariot of the baby gods

A GOD IS BORN

Jealous Hera throws a fit, but a little island saves the day.

Apollo and his twin sister, Artemis, were born on the island of Delos, the only place that would allow their mother, Leto, to give birth. That's because Zeus was their daddy, which didn't please his wife, the goddess Hera, at all! In fact she forbade the birth to take place on land or anywhere the sun shone. Fortunately Poseidon, the god of the sea and Apollo's uncle, revealed a small bit of the island that had been covered with water (the Greek word *delos* means "visible"). As soon as Apollo was born, he was fed **nectar** and **ambrosia**, and within a day he had become a full-grown god!

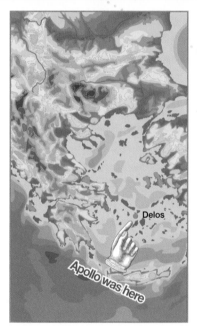

Delos

Apollo was here

REALITY CHECK

Is there really an island of Delos? Yes! Delos is in the Aegean Sea, near the island of Mykonos. The Greeks considered it sacred and built temples and statues there honoring the gods.

Want to know more? Go to: whc.unesco.org/

Apollo

Python

Python was born out of the slime after a major flood in Delphi.

Daphne

THE ORACLE AT DELPHI

Apollo finds a spot for his temple, slays a dragon, and sets up shop at Delphi.

As the god of **prophecy**, or predicting the future, Apollo needed a temple where **mortals** could ask him questions. Apollo's answers would be spoken through an **oracle**, or **prophet**. He found the perfect spot at Pytho—well, perfect after he killed a horrible dragon that lived there. Apollo's answers were spoken through the Pythia, or priestess of the temple. Pytho later came to be known as Delphi.

The sacred area of Apollo's temple was home to:

➤ a golden statue of Apollo
➤ the **omphalos**
➤ the supposed tomb of the god Dionysus
➤ a deep **chasm**, on top of which sat a **tripod**

The Pythia sat on the tripod, drinking water from a nearby sacred spring, chewing laurel leaves, and shaking a laurel branch.

REALITY CHECK

The ruins of Apollo's temple at Delphi can still be seen today on the slopes of Mount Parnassus in Greece.

Want to know more? Go to:
www.ancient-greece.org/architecture/delphi-temple-of-apollo.html

HIDE AND SEEK

Daphne makes like a tree and leaves—for good!

Apollo was madly in love with the **nymph** Daphne, but she didn't feel the same way. Eros, the naughty god of love, had shot Apollo with a golden arrow to make him feel lovey-dovey, and shot Daphne with a lead arrow so she'd say "NO WAY." One day Apollo followed Daphne to the banks of the River Peneus. As Apollo reached toward her, Daphne cried to her father, a river god, for help. Suddenly she turned into a laurel tree! Apollo swore on the spot that he'd always love Daphne. To prove it, he wore a laurel wreath on his head forever.

Temple of Apollo at Delphi

Eros

"I like to pluck a tune on the lyre while the Muses sing and dance!"

BATTLE OF THE BANDS

Marsyas challenges Apollo to a contest and is hung out to dry.

The **satyr** Marsyas challenged Apollo to a musical contest. The winner could do what he wished with the loser. Apollo played his **lyre** like a god and won—and poor Marsyas, who played the pipes, was hung from a tree and skinned aive.

Satyrs are half-man, half-goat. They love to frolic in the forest and chase nymphs.

Satyr

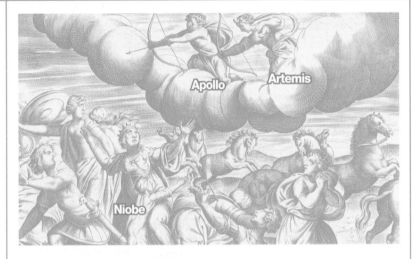

Apollo Artemis

Niobe

APOLLO AND NIOBE

Niobe makes an unwise boast, and Apollo and Artemis stick up for their mom.

The **mortal** Niobe boasted that she was equal to Leto, the mother of Apollo and Artemis, because she had given birth to many children while Leto had borne only two. Big mistake! Her boast enraged Apollo and Artemis, who retaliated by using their bows and arrows to kill all 14 of Niobe's children; Apollo shot the boys and Artemis shot the girls.

Crazed with grief, Niobe was put out of her misery by Zeus, who turned her into a rock. But even that didn't stop her from crying! Out of the rock came the Achelous, a stream fed by her ceaseless tears.

REALITY CHECK

Niobe became the symbol of eternal mourning. On a rock cliff on Mount Sipylus, nature has carved the image of a female that the Greeks claim is Niobe. The stone is said to weep even to this day.

Want to know more? Go to:
www.1911encyclopedia.org/Niobe

She weeps all day!

Niobe

"My twin sister, Artemis, and I invented hunting—just ask Niobe!"

AGAMEMNON'S INSULT

A hero makes a cowardly mistake.

In another story, Apollo used his skill as an archer to show his power over sickness and healing. This time the hero Agamemnon, commander in chief of the Greeks during the Trojan War, insulted an elderly priest of Apollo. The old priest prayed to Apollo, asking him to make the Greeks pay for this insult. Apollo obliged by coming down from Olympus for nine days and shooting poison arrows at the mules, hounds, and men in the Greek camp, infecting them with a plague.

> "As the god of sickness and healing, sometimes I heal people— and sometimes I make them sick."

UNLUCKY IN LOVE

Apollo gives Cassandra the gift that keeps on giving.

A glutton for punishment, Apollo fell in love with the princess Cassandra, the beautiful daughter of Priam, king of Troy, and Hecuba. To prove his love, Apollo gave Cassandra the gift of **prophecy**. But when she rejected him, Apollo cursed her so that no one would believe a word she said. Cassandra foretold the downfall of Troy and warned about the dangers of the Trojan Horse, but no one believed her. Later she warned Agamemnon upon his return from the war that his unfaithful wife Clytemnestra was going to kill him. Agamemnon didn't believe her, but Cassandra was right again. Clytemnestra and her boyfriend Aegisthus killed Agamemnon and Cassandra.

Phone message text:
hey A-
not sure how 2 say this...
it's not u, it's me. i
totally<3 having the gift
of prophecy (thanx again!)
but...ur just not the god 4
me. sorry...
Cassandra

Clytemnestra

murder weapon

REALITY CHECK

The legendary struggle known as the Trojan War took place between the people of Greece and the people of Troy. It was the setting for Homer's epic *The Iliad*. But was it real? Archaeologists uncovered evidence that the real Troy had been sacked around 1250 BCE.

Don't mess with a princess!

Where are the windows in this thing?

Trojan Horse

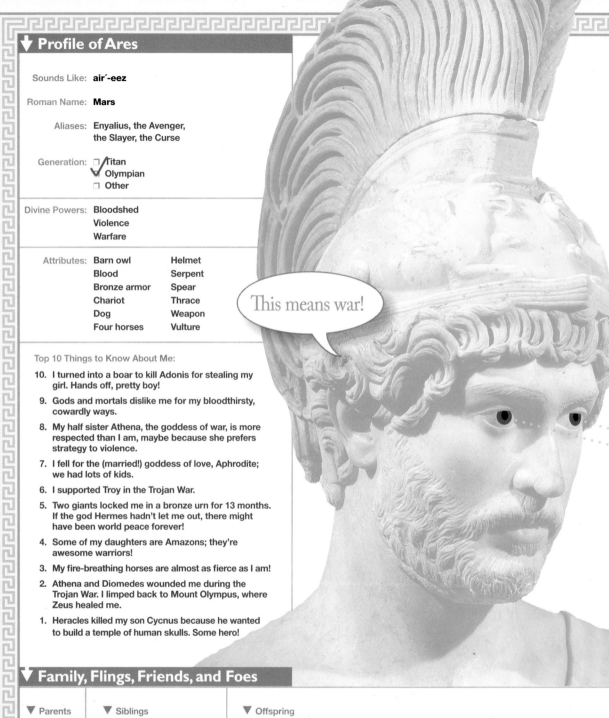

↓ Profile of Ares

Sounds Like: **air´-eez**

Roman Name: **Mars**

Aliases: Enyalius, the Avenger, the Slayer, the Curse

Generation: ☐ Titan
☑ Olympian
☐ Other

Divine Powers: Bloodshed
Violence
Warfare

Attributes:

Barn owl	Helmet
Blood	Serpent
Bronze armor	Spear
Chariot	Thrace
Dog	Weapon
Four horses	Vulture

This means war!

Top 10 Things to Know About Me:

10. I turned into a boar to kill Adonis for stealing my girl. Hands off, pretty boy!

9. Gods and mortals dislike me for my bloodthirsty, cowardly ways.

8. My half sister Athena, the goddess of war, is more respected than I am, maybe because she prefers strategy to violence.

7. I fell for the (married!) goddess of love, Aphrodite; we had lots of kids.

6. I supported Troy in the Trojan War.

5. Two giants locked me in a bronze urn for 13 months. If the god Hermes hadn't let me out, there might have been world peace forever!

4. Some of my daughters are Amazons; they're awesome warriors!

3. My fire-breathing horses are almost as fierce as I am!

2. Athena and Diomedes wounded me during the Trojan War. I limped back to Mount Olympus, where Zeus healed me.

1. Heracles killed my son Cycnus because he wanted to build a temple of human skulls. Some hero!

▼ Family, Flings, Friends, and Foes

▼ Parents	▼ Siblings		▼ Offspring				
Zeus and Hera	Eris	Hephaestus	Deimos	Phobos	Cycnus	Eros	Hippolyte

ARES

MAKE WAR, NOT LOVE

Listen up, Athena: Mount Olympus only has room for one war deity—me! Your "strategic battle" thing is garbage. War is what I live for! I don't care who's wrong or right, as long as I get my war on. And those rumors about my being a coward are lies. I may not be Mr. Popularity, but Aphrodite picked me to be her boyfriend. She can't be wrong! So back off, Athena, and leave the warmongering to a gore-lovin' god like me.

Athena

Talk to the hand, Ares.

▼ Flings

 Aphrodite

 Enyo

 Eos

▼ Friends

 Hector

 Hermes

▼ Foes

 The Aloadae

 Helios

Adonis

23

ARES

"Let's get ready to rumble."

MYTH LOPEDIA

Αρης

> "I can be a real animal when I need to be ... just ask Adonis!"

IT'S GREEK TO ME

Mars was the Roman equivalent of Ares, but with a twist. Both were gods of war, but Mars was also the god of agriculture, a role filled in Greek mythology by the goddess Demeter. And like Athena, who was so important to Athens, Mars was particularly important to Rome. In fact, he was regarded as the father of the Roman people and had several temples dedicated to him.

WHAT A BOAR!

Ares "boars" a rival suitor to death.

It wasn't enough for bloodthirsty Ares to murder with his spear, or even his bare hands— sometimes he killed by **transfiguring** himself into a wild animal! When his ex-girlfriend Aphrodite started dating the handsome **mortal** Adonis, Ares was so consumed with jealousy that he followed Adonis into the forest. There he turned himself into a **venomous** boar with razor-sharp tusks. Wild with rage, he attacked, using his tusks to rip holes in Adonis's body. Aphrodite heard the mortal's moans and rushed to save him, but she arrived too late— Adonis died in her arms.

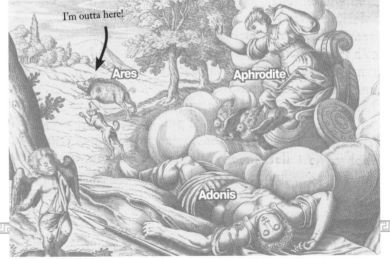

I'm outta here!

Ares

Aphrodite

Adonis

The gods saw the whole thing!

"Heph"

Net

Ares

Aphrodite

ALL'S FAIR IN LOVE

Hephaestus sets a trap and nets a pair of cheaters!

Zeus made Aphrodite marry Hephaestus, but he couldn't force her to be faithful. The goddess of love fell head over heels for Ares. When Helios, god of the sun and a notorious tattletale, saw Aphrodite canoodling with Ares, he told Hephaestus everything. Hephaestus made a net of nearly invisible gold links to trap the lovers. The next time Ares and Aphrodite were together—snap! Caught in the act!

Hephaestus invited all the gods from Olympus to see the guilty pair. While he raged about his unfaithful wife, the gods laughed at the lovers.

"Those giants should pick on someone their own size!"

A GIANT BATTLE

Giant ambitions "urn" Ares some time out.

A pair of twin giants, the Aloadae, had ambitions that were almost as big as their bodies. They believed that they could take over Mount Olympus and destroy the Olympians. They planned to stack three tall mountains on top of one another, so that they could climb up to Olympus. Ares tried to stop them, but he was no match for their brute strength. The Aloadae chained him up and threw him into a bronze urn, where he stayed for 13 months until Hermes rescued him. Apollo then killed the giants before they did any more damage.

Those teachers just "boar" me!

THE FAMILY THAT SLAYS TOGETHER, STAYS TOGETHER

Ares' family members are just as violent as he is.

Ares passed on his bloodthirsty nature to many of his children. His sons Deimos (god of terror) and Phobos (god of fear) spread terror and fear across the land. His son Cycnus tried to build a temple out of human bones and skulls! His sister Eris was the goddess of discord, and the war goddess Enyo—with whom he had a child—might also have been his sister. And at least one of his daughters was an Amazon, a group of famed female warriors.

From: Principal@MountOlympusSchool.edu
Re: Parent-Teacher Conference

Dear Ares and Aphrodite,

The new school year has just begun, and your sons Deimos, Phobos, and Cycnus have already started terrorizing students on the playground. I remind you that Mount Olympus School has a zero-tolerance policy regarding bullying. Please contact my secretary to arrange a parent-teacher conference.
    Sincerely yours,

    The Principal

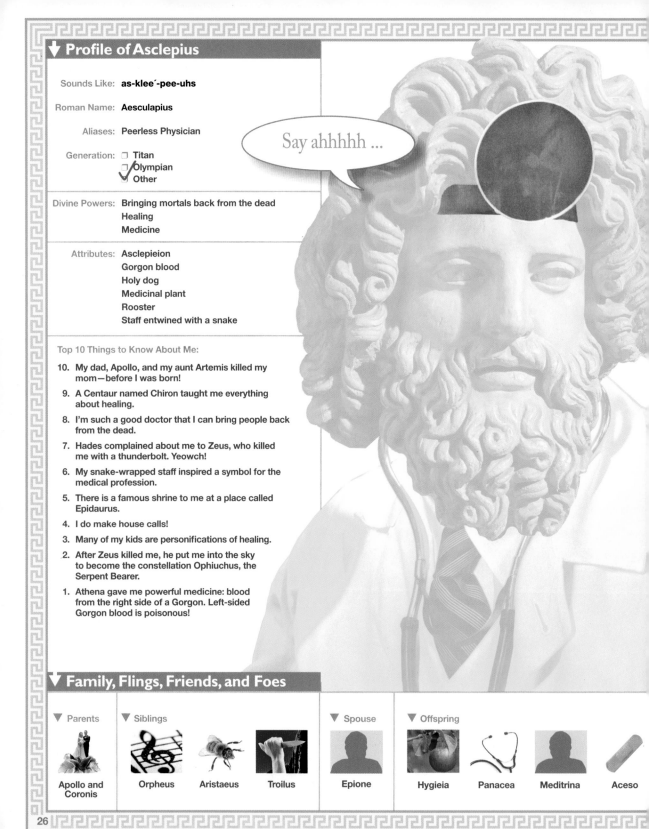

▼ Profile of Asclepius

Sounds Like: **as-klee´-pee-uhs**

Roman Name: **Aesculapius**

Aliases: Peerless Physician

Generation: ☐ Titan
☐ Olympian
☑ Other

Divine Powers: Bringing mortals back from the dead
Healing
Medicine

Attributes: Asclepieion
Gorgon blood
Holy dog
Medicinal plant
Rooster
Staff entwined with a snake

Say ahhhh ...

Top 10 Things to Know About Me:

10. My dad, Apollo, and my aunt Artemis killed my mom—before I was born!

9. A Centaur named Chiron taught me everything about healing.

8. I'm such a good doctor that I can bring people back from the dead.

7. Hades complained about me to Zeus, who killed me with a thunderbolt. Yeowch!

6. My snake-wrapped staff inspired a symbol for the medical profession.

5. There is a famous shrine to me at a place called Epidaurus.

4. I do make house calls!

3. Many of my kids are personifications of healing.

2. After Zeus killed me, he put me into the sky to become the constellation Ophiuchus, the Serpent Bearer.

1. Athena gave me powerful medicine: blood from the right side of a Gorgon. Left-sided Gorgon blood is poisonous!

▼ Family, Flings, Friends, and Foes

▼ **Parents**

Apollo and Coronis

▼ **Siblings**

Orpheus

Aristaeus

Troilus

▼ **Spouse**

Epione

▼ **Offspring**

Hygieia

Panacea

Meditrina

Aceso

ASCLEPIUS

LET ME HEAL YOU

Heal thyself with *Dr. Asclepius's Guide to Great Health*. Learn about: Snakes and Their Healing Powers; Sacred Dogs Who Lick Away Wounds; and Dreaming Your Way to Health! Includes the top Asclepieions and the goddesses to know for healing help (hint: they're my kids!). First 50 callers receive a bonus—a vial of Gorgon blood, guaranteed to provide a second chance at life. Great for when Thanatos visits!

Disclaimer: *This book is not intended to diagnose, treat, or cure any disease or illness.*

This won't hurt a bit.

				▼ Friends	▼ Foes		
Iaso	Machaon	Podalirius		Chiron	Athena	Hades	Zeus

ASCLEPIUS

"An apple a day keeps the doctor away."

MYTH LOPEDIA

Ασκληπιος

Coronis

IT'S GREEK TO ME

Have you ever wondered why the **caduceus**, a staff with two entwining snakes, is the symbol for medicine? Look to Asclepius, who carried a staff with one snake wrapped around it. Later, another snake was added for symmetry.

BORN IN FIRE

Asclepius gets off to a hot start in life.

Asclepius's mom, Coronis, was a beautiful **mortal** who had a passionate affair with Apollo. Then she made a terrible mistake. While pregnant with Apollo's son Asclepius, Coronis fell in love with another man. When Apollo found out, he was so furious that he ordered his sister, Artemis, to kill Coronis!

After Coronis was murdered, her body was placed on a funeral **pyre**, which was lit on fire. Apollo cut Asclepius from Coronis's smoldering body. No wonder the little guy grew up with a strong interest in medicine!

REALITY CHECK

Cremation is used by many cultures to dispose of their dead. The deceased is burned on a pyre or in a crematory, and the ashes may be disposed of ritually.

"Chiron the Centaur raised me—and taught me all his secrets!"

THE CENTAUR CONNECTION

Apollo hires a babysitter.

After Apollo rescued Asclepius from Coronis's body, he had to find someone to raise the motherless baby. (Apparently Apollo was too busy to do it himself.) Apollo picked just the right babysitter: a **Centaur** named Chiron. Most Centaurs were rude creatures who partied hard, but Chiron was surprisingly kind, compassionate, and wise. He also had amazing healing skills, which he taught to the young Asclepius. With the blood of Apollo coursing through his veins and the knowledge of Chiron stored in his mind, Asclepius was destined to become the greatest healer the world has ever known.

Chiron

Hygieia

Asclepius

MEDICAL MAIDENS

Asclepius's daughters follow in their daddy's footsteps and practice the art of healing.

Asclepius's daughters became healers like their dad—and even inspired many of the words we use about medicine. His daughter Hygieia was the goddess of health (and her name is related to the English word *hygiene*, which means "cleanliness"). Iaso was the goddess of recovery, and Aceso was the goddess of healing. Panacea was the goddess of cures—and even today, her name means "cure-all" in English.

Is there a doctor in the house?

Dead Guy

DON'T DIS DEATH

An outraged Hades demands Asclepius's death.

Asclepius was such an amazing doctor that he could cure any disease—and even bring people back from the dead! The goddess Athena had given Asclepius a **vial** of blood from a monstrous Gorgon that could restore life to those who had died. This enraged Hades, the god of the **Underworld**, who believed that the souls of the dead belonged to him—and him alone.

Hades complained to Zeus, who treated the problem as he usually handled minor annoyances: by zapping Asclepius with a thunderbolt. Asclepius was killed instantly. Apollo was so angry at Zeus for killing Asclepius that he killed the Cyclopes who had crafted Zeus's thunderbolts. To show his appreciation for Asclepius's skills (and perhaps to make amends with Apollo), Zeus turned Asclepius into a constellation—Ophiuchus, the Serpent Bearer.

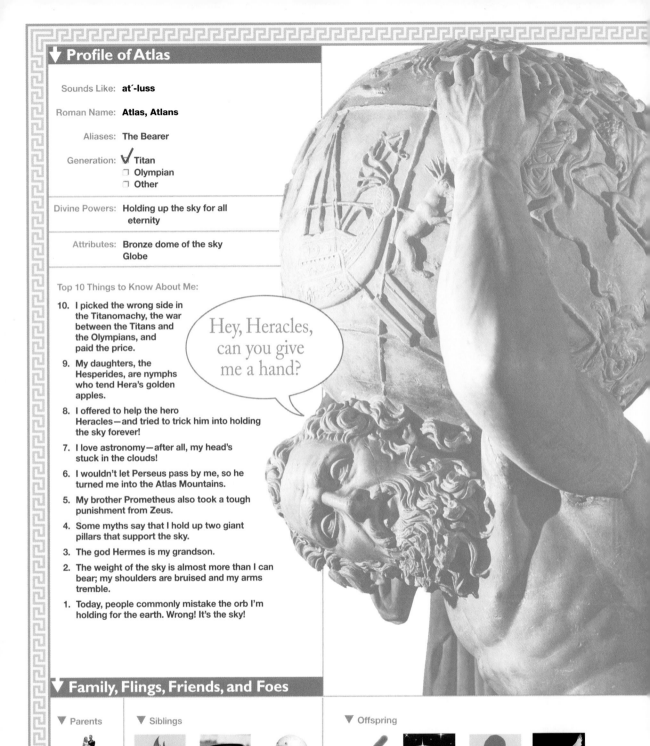

▼ Profile of Atlas

Sounds Like:	**at´-luss**
Roman Name:	**Atlas, Atlans**
Aliases:	**The Bearer**
Generation:	✓ **Titan**
	☐ **Olympian**
	☐ **Other**
Divine Powers:	**Holding up the sky for all eternity**
Attributes:	**Bronze dome of the sky**
	Globe

Top 10 Things to Know About Me:

10. I picked the wrong side in the Titanomachy, the war between the Titans and the Olympians, and paid the price.

9. My daughters, the Hesperides, are nymphs who tend Hera's golden apples.

8. I offered to help the hero Heracles—and tried to trick him into holding the sky forever!

7. I love astronomy—after all, my head's stuck in the clouds!

6. I wouldn't let Perseus pass by me, so he turned me into the Atlas Mountains.

5. My brother Prometheus also took a tough punishment from Zeus.

4. Some myths say that I hold up two giant pillars that support the sky.

3. The god Hermes is my grandson.

2. The weight of the sky is almost more than I can bear; my shoulders are bruised and my arms tremble.

1. Today, people commonly mistake the orb I'm holding for the earth. Wrong! It's the sky!

Hey, Heracles, can you give me a hand?

▼ Family, Flings, Friends, and Foes

▼ Parents	▼ Siblings			▼ Offspring			
Iapetus and Clymene	Prometheus	Epimetheus	Menoetius	The Hesperides	The Pleiades	Calypso	Dione

ATLAS
HELP WANTED

Strong, silent type to hold sky on shoulders. Duties: standing still and not complaining about this awful job. This is a temporary position. I promise I will return and take back the incredibly heavy sky. Really. Seriously, you'd be doing me a huge favor if you'd hold the sky for an hour. Two hours, most. I just want to grab an apple. Flexible schedule. Calloused hands a plus. Apply to Atlas at the far end of the world.

Sorry, I've got my hands full!

Heracles

▼ Flings

Hesperis   **Pleione**

▼ Friends

Heracles

▼ Foes

Zeus   **Perseus**

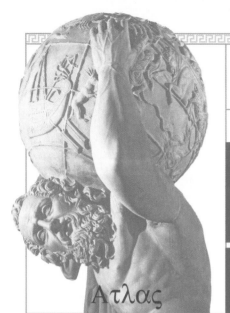

Ατλας

ATLAS

"Oh, my achin' back ..."

MYTHLOPEDIA

It's a big job!

Atlas

"One mistake and Zeus sticks me with holding up the sky for eternity— no fair!"

IT'S GREEK TO ME

The ancient Greeks thought the sky was a dome suspended above the earth, so their art shows Atlas holding a globe. Today, people often mistake this globe for the earth, and think Atlas's job was to hold up the earth instead of the sky.

REACH FOR THE SKY—FOREVER!

Atlas picks the wrong side in the Titanomachy, and Zeus punishes him— big time!

Atlas was the son of Iapetus, one of the original 12 Titans who ruled before Zeus started the Titanomachy. This ten-year war between the Titans and Olympians decided who would rule heaven and earth. Atlas had to make a choice: join his family in the fight, or side with Zeus—and betray his blood. Atlas stuck with the Titans, which proved to be a big mistake. After Zeus led the Olympians to victory, the Titans who had sided against him were severely punished: Zeus threw them into the darkest depths of Tartarus, deep within the **Underworld**. But not Atlas. He got a special punishment from Zeus. He was forced to hold up the enormous sky, Uranus, forever. With a punishment like that, Atlas probably wished that he'd betrayed his family after all!

GOING FOR THE GOLD

Atlas tries to trick Heracles, but the hero has a trick of his own.

For Atlas, carrying the entire heavens on his shoulders must have become exhausting after the first several years or so. No wonder he was eager to trick someone into taking over his enormous job! Meanwhile, heroic Heracles had a big job of his own: He was charged with the task of collecting the goddess Hera's golden apples, which were tended by the Hesperides. The Hesperides were Atlas's daughters, so Heracles thought that Atlas could help him. Atlas, however, had a plan of his own. He offered to get the apples for Heracles—as long as Heracles would hold up the sky while he was gone. Atlas had no intention of taking back the sky, but Heracles was one step ahead of him. When Atlas returned with the apples, Heracles asked him to hold the sky for a moment while he adjusted his cloak to make holding the sky a little more comfortable. Tricked! As soon as Atlas took the sky, Heracles grabbed the apples and ran! And Atlas was once again stuck holding up the sky for all eternity.

A MOUNTAIN OF TROUBLE

A rude Titan is set in stone.

The hero Perseus was exhausted. He had just killed monstrous Medusa, a hideous Gorgon, almost dying in the process. As night fell, Perseus politely asked Atlas for permission to rest in his lands. But Atlas feared that Perseus would steal his golden apples, so he refused to show the hero the common courtesy that all travelers deserve. Perseus couldn't tolerate such rudeness. He showed Medusa's **severed** head to Atlas and *bam*! The mighty Titan instantly turned to stone and became the Atlas Mountain range.

REALITY CHECK

The Atlas Mountains are a system of mountain ranges and plateaus in North Africa that extend across Morocco, Algeria, and Tunisia.

Atlas Mountains

▼ Profile of Cronus

Sounds Like: **kroh´-nuhs**

Roman Name: **Saturn**

Generation: ✓ Titan
☐ Olympian
☐ Other

Divine Powers: **Leader of the Titans**

Attributes: **Sickle**

Top 10 Things to Know About Me:

10. I'm the youngest of the Titans.

9. I mutilated my dad, Uranus, and took power!

8. After I heard that one of my kids would overthrow me, I swallowed them when they were born.

7. When my son Zeus was born, my wife hid him and gave me a wrapped-up rock to swallow instead.

6. Zeus slipped me a drink that made me throw up all his siblings. UGH!

5. When Zeus grew up, he started a war called the Titanomachy to overthrow me. It took ten years, but he won!

4. Zeus punished me by throwing me into Tartarus, the worst part of the entire Underworld, with a lot of other Titans.

3. My own mom helped my wife protect Zeus and overthrow me. Thanks for nothing, Mom!

2. My rule was called the Golden Age; it was a time of peace and plenty for humans.

1. After hundreds of years, Zeus freed me from Tartarus and let me be king of Elysia, the Isles of the Blessed.

> Mmm mmm good!

▼ Family, Flings, Friends, and Foes

▼ Parents	▼ Siblings	▼ Spouse	▼ Offspring					
Uranus and Gaea	Other Titans	Rhea	Zeus	Hades	Poseidon	Demeter	Hestia	Hera

CRONUS

GO TITANS!

Huddle up, Titans. We've been through a lot together—first with Mom and Dad, then those years of prison in Tartarus. But that was all training for right now: our showdown with Zeus. (I should have swallowed him when I had the chance.) The Olympians don't respect us. But we're gonna show those newbies who rules around here. Am I right? I said, am I right? I CAN'T HEAR YOU! YEAH! Now get out there and eat 'em alive!

> Stop eating the kids or you'll spoil your appetite!

▼ Foes

Zeus

Prometheus

Gaea

His children

Rhea

CRONUS

"My tummy hurts!"

MYTHLOPEDIA

"You've got to be cruel to be kind ... especially if you're hungry!"

IT'S GREEK TO ME

The Titans were the 12 offspring of Uranus (Sky) and Gaea (Earth). They include Oceanus, the stream surrounding the world; Coeus; Crius; Hyperion; Iapetus; Theia; Themis; Mnemosyne; Phoebe; Tethys; and Rhea and Cronus, parents of the original Olympian gods.

Titans

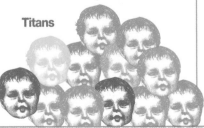

TAKE THAT, TYRANT!

Cronus teaches his dad the worst kind of lesson.

Uranus and Gaea were two of the very first gods and were also **personifications** of the sky (Uranus) and the earth (Gaea). Their offspring included the hundred-handed Hecatoncheires, the one-eyed Cyclopes, and the mighty Titans.

Uranus was sickened and frightened by his monstrous offspring. He worried that they would overthrow him, so he imprisoned them in Tartarus, the bleakest realm of the **Underworld**, deep inside the earth. This caused Gaea terrible pain, so she plotted against Uranus, convincing her Titan son

Cronus attacked his dad with a sickle. OUCH!

Cronus to attack his dad with a sickle.

After the attack, Cronus threw Uranus's body parts into the sea. As the leader of this brutal attack, Cronus then became the ruler of the gods ... for a while.

"I showed my dad what happens to bullies on the pantheon playground!"

LIKE FATHER, LIKE SON

Cronus follows in his dad's paranoid footsteps.

After he became the most powerful god, Cronus married his sister Rhea. But when Uranus and Gaea foresaw that one of Cronus's children would overthrow him, Cronus became just as suspicious of his kids as Uranus had been of his. Cronus tried to prevent the **prophecy**, or prediction, from coming true by keeping his children from growing up. So Cronus gulped down each child as it was born, one by one! That was too much for Rhea, and she hatched a plot with Gaea to trick Cronus. When Rhea's sixth child, Zeus, was born, she put the plan into motion. Rhea handed Cronus a rock wrapped in a baby blanket and hid little Zeus on the island of Crete. Cronus swallowed the rock, never suspecting that one of his children was in the world, waiting to overthrow him. When Zeus grew up, he disguised himself as Cronus's **cupbearer** and added a **potion** to his father's drink that made Cronus vomit up each one of his siblings. Zeus was reunited with his powerful brothers and sisters, and the event that Cronus had most feared came to pass—a war for ultimate power between the Titans and the Olympians, called the Titanomachy.

Kids! They're what's for dinner!

TITANS VS.

The Hecatoncheires gave the Olympians a hand.

OLYMPIANS

Zeus used his thunderbolts to lead the Olympians to victory.

Joe, we've got an ugly match-up here—literally. Look at those monsters. Both teams are in it to win. With Zeus leading the O-Team offense, we're gonna see some thunderbolts. What's that? Cyclops just ate a Titan defender! Man, that's gotta hurt.

Don't mess with the god of the Underworld.

With the weight of the sky on his shoulders, Atlas supported the Titans.

TEAM TITAN

Trading cards...

TETHYS

COEUS

COACH
CRONUS

HYPERION

CRIUS

IAPETUS

RHEA

PHOEBE

ATLAS

MNEMOSYNE

THEIA

OCEANUS

HADES

DEMETER

COACH

ZEUS

HECATONCHEIRES

HERA

ATHENA

TEAM
OLYMPIAN

collect them all...

POSEIDON

PROMETHEUS

CYCLOPS

ARTEMIS

HERMES

ARES

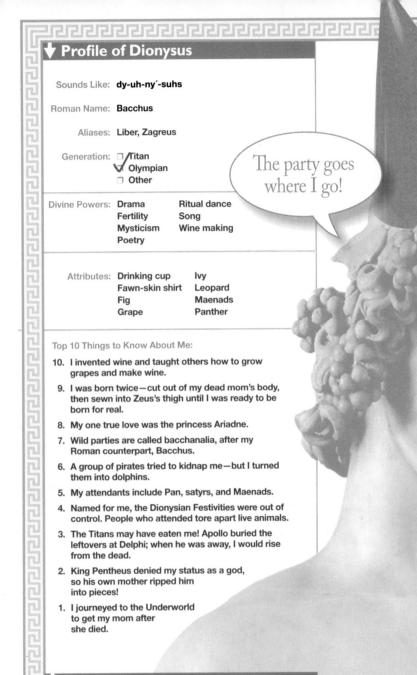

Profile of Dionysus

Sounds Like: dy-uh-ny´-suhs

Roman Name: Bacchus

Aliases: Liber, Zagreus

Generation:
- ☐ Titan
- ☑ Olympian
- ☐ Other

Divine Powers: Drama, Fertility, Mysticism, Poetry, Ritual dance, Song, Wine making

Attributes: Drinking cup, Fawn-skin shirt, Fig, Grape, Ivy, Leopard, Maenads, Panther

The party goes where I go!

Top 10 Things to Know About Me:

10. I invented wine and taught others how to grow grapes and make wine.

9. I was born twice—cut out of my dead mom's body, then sewn into Zeus's thigh until I was ready to be born for real.

8. My one true love was the princess Ariadne.

7. Wild parties are called bacchanalia, after my Roman counterpart, Bacchus.

6. A group of pirates tried to kidnap me—but I turned them into dolphins.

5. My attendants include Pan, satyrs, and Maenads.

4. Named for me, the Dionysian Festivities were out of control. People who attended tore apart live animals.

3. The Titans may have eaten me! Apollo buried the leftovers at Delphi; when he was away, I would rise from the dead.

2. King Pentheus denied my status as a god, so his own mother ripped him into pieces!

1. I journeyed to the Underworld to get my mom after she died.

Family, Flings, Friends, and Foes

▼ **Parents**

Zeus and Semele

▼ **Siblings**

Apollo

Ares

Artemis

Hermes

Persephone

Heracles

▼ **Spouse**

Ariadne

▼ **Offsp**

Thoas

DIONYSUS
PARTY ON!

You're invited to the PARTY OF THE YEAR—the City Dionysia—an off-the-hook celebration starring everyone's favorite god-gone-wild, me! Join my girl Ariadne and me in Athens this March for crazy choruses, heartbreaking tragedies, bawdy comedies, festive parades, and rioting in the streets. Remember, it's BYO bread, wine, pigs, and bulls! C'mon now. Let's get this party started!

REALITY CHECK

In Greece you can attend theater festivals in the tradition of the City Dionysia. Every year, in the ancient theater at Epidaurus, the works of such great Greek playwrights as Euripides, Sophocles, and Aeschylus are presented.

Want to know more? Go to:
http://www.greekfestival.gr

> Party's on my page, D! Come on over!

Pan

▼ Friends

| Oenopion | Staphylus | Pan | Satyrs | Maenads |

▼ Foes

| Pentheus | Hera | Titans | Tyrrhenian pirates |

"Let's get this party started!"

MYTHLOPEDIA

Διονυσος

IT'S GREEK TO ME

Dionysia festivals honor the god Dionysus. The City Dionysia was held in Athens, Greece, for six days near the end of March. It began with a procession that carried a statue of the god to various temples, with singing and sacrifices, and ended in the theater of Dionysus at the Acropolis. The celebration included productions of tragedies, satyr plays, and comedies.

Comedy   **Tragedy**

TWICE-BORN GOD

Dionysus is not quite ready for prime time when he makes his first appearance in the world.

Dionysus was the son of the god Zeus and the **mortal** Semele. Zeus's jealous wife, Hera, wanted revenge against Semele, so she disguised herself as a nurse and visited Semele, who was pregnant with Dionysus. Hera wickedly caused Semele to doubt that Zeus was actually the father of her child, suggesting the father might have been a trickster pretending to be Zeus!

Semele decided to ask Zeus for a favor. He promised her anything, so she insisted that Zeus show himself in his real form—as a god. Zeus begged her to change her mind, for a mortal who saw an undisguised god would die a horrible death.

But Semele insisted, and Zeus couldn't go back on his word. Sure enough, when he came to her cloaked in lightning bolts, Semele burst into flames. Zeus rescued the unborn Dionysus from Semele's burning body and sewed the baby into his thigh so that Dionysus could keep growing until he was ready to be born.

"I was a little underdone, so my dad tucked me in his thigh to keep cooking!"

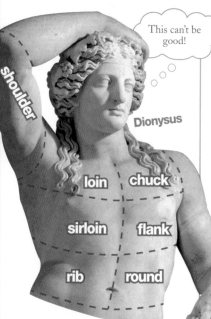

This can't be good!

shoulder

Dionysus

loin | chuck

sirloin | flank

rib | round

DIONYSUS FOR DINNER

Hera serves up a feast that the Titans can't resist.

Hera's destruction of Semele wasn't the last trouble she made for Dionysus. She wanted to eliminate him—even when he was a baby! So she convinced the Titans to attack him. They ripped Dionysus into pieces, roasted him, and ate him. When Zeus discovered what they had done, he rescued some of the parts of Dionysus and had them buried at Apollo's temple. Whenever Apollo was away from his temple, Dionysus would rise up and rule. In another version of the story, Rhea rescued the pieces of Dionysus and made him whole—and alive—again.

A BUNCH OF GRAPES

Dionysus loses his mind, hits the road, and discovers his green thumb.

After Dionysus emerged from Zeus's thigh, he was raised by **nymphs** to keep him safe from Hera's wrath. But even years later, Hera wanted revenge for Zeus's infidelity, so she cursed Dionysus with madness that forced him to wander the world. During his voyages, Dionysus discovered how to grow grapes—and how to turn them into wine. This skill gave his travels a new purpose. Instead of wandering the world as a madman, Dionysus journeyed near and far to teach people how to grow grapes and make wine from them—and to encourage mortals to worship him.

"Oh, I heard it through the grapevine…"

REALITY CHECK

Growing and cultivating grapes for wine production is known as viticulture. Grape vines were introduced in Greece long before the fall of Troy (1184 BCE). Along with olives and grain, grapes were an important crop in ancient Greece.

Want to know more? Go to: www.greekproducts.com/greekproducts/wine/history.html

Hey, D—may I have a couple of those grapes? They look good!

TRUE LOVE

Dionysus meets and marries the princess of his dreams.

Dionysus had one true love: the lovely **mortal** princess Ariadne. Before meeting Dionysus, Ariadne had fallen in love with a prince named Theseus and helped him escape from the Minotaur, a terrible monster that lived in a **maze**. Ariadne ran off with Theseus, who later abandoned her on the island of Naxos. The goddess of love, Aphrodite, tried to comfort the brokenhearted princess by

D-dude, u gotta do something about those maenads. 4 real, those ladies are off the hook! totally wack! my dad is gonna freak when he sees what they did to the Minotaur. I mean, OUCH.

promising that she would find even greater love. It just so happened that Naxos was one of Dionysus's favorite places, and the god found the lovelorn Ariadne there. He instantly fell in love with her, and the two were married—making Aphrodite's promise come true.

REALITY CHECK
Naxos is one of the Cyclades Islands. It is in the Aegean Sea, off the coast of Greece. Its chief town is also called Naxos.

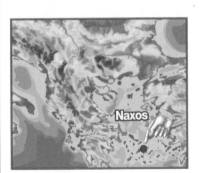

Naxos

MAENAD MADNESS

These women are crazy for Dionysus—literally!

The Maenads were a group of women who worshipped Dionysus. They were completely wild and out of control as they traveled from festival to festival, drinking, dancing, and wreaking havoc. Dressed in animal skins, carrying thyrsi (ivy-covered staffs topped with pine cones), and crowned with wreaths of ivy, the Maenads were frightening figures. In their insanity, they would rip apart and devour live animals. They were even known to kill humans!

Killer plants?

Maenad

SOMETHING FISHY

Dionysus makes pirates walk the plank!

During his travels, Dionysus sometimes tried to disguise himself as an ordinary mortal. But this plan backfired when a group of pirates spied the handsome, well-dressed god and mistook him for a nobleman. They kidnapped Dionysus, planning to ransom him for a large sum of money. Only one of the sailors saw through Dionysus's disguise to the god hidden within, and he urged the others to let the **deity** go and beg his forgiveness.

Blinded by greed, the other pirates refused to do so—and paid the price! Soon vines of ivy, heavy with grapes, grew over the ship, and Dionysus turned himself into a ferocious lion. Terrified, the pirates jumped overboard and were instantly turned into dolphins! The only one spared was the pirate who had thought Dionysus was a god to begin with.

AARGH!
A pirate's life for me! ....

DON'T DENY DIONYSUS

Dionysus dishes out revenge to Pentheus.

Few things angered Dionysus more than when people refused to believe that he was a god—or even worse, refused to worship him! Pentheus, the king of Thebes, stubbornly refused to acknowledge Dionysus's greatness, and he threatened to kill Dionysus's followers. When his threats did nothing to persuade mortals to abandon Dionysus, Pentheus charged into the woods to the **Dionysia** to confront Dionysus. Pentheus's mother, Agave, was one of the Maenads there. Like the others, Agave was in a wild frenzy. When she looked at her son, Agave didn't see a human, she saw a wild lion. So she led a charge to attack it! The Maenads ripped Pentheus to pieces. From then on, there was no further resistance to the worship of Dionysus in Greece.

"I don't get mad; I get even!"

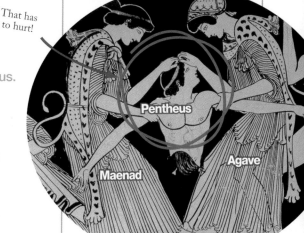

That has to hurt!

Pentheus

Maenad

Agave

MAKING THE O-TEAM

A favor for a goddess pays off big-time.

When Hera's son Hephaestus was born, he was so ugly that his mother threw him off Mount Olympus. This caused the poor ugly baby to become lame. Hephaestus, the god of blacksmithing, became a master craftsman and made a gift for his mother: a trick throne that trapped her when she sat down in it.

Because only Hephaestus could release Hera, Dionysus gave the god some wine and convinced him to return to Olympus and set his mother free. In gratitude, Hera accepted Dionysus as an Olympian and persuaded the other Olympians to do the same.

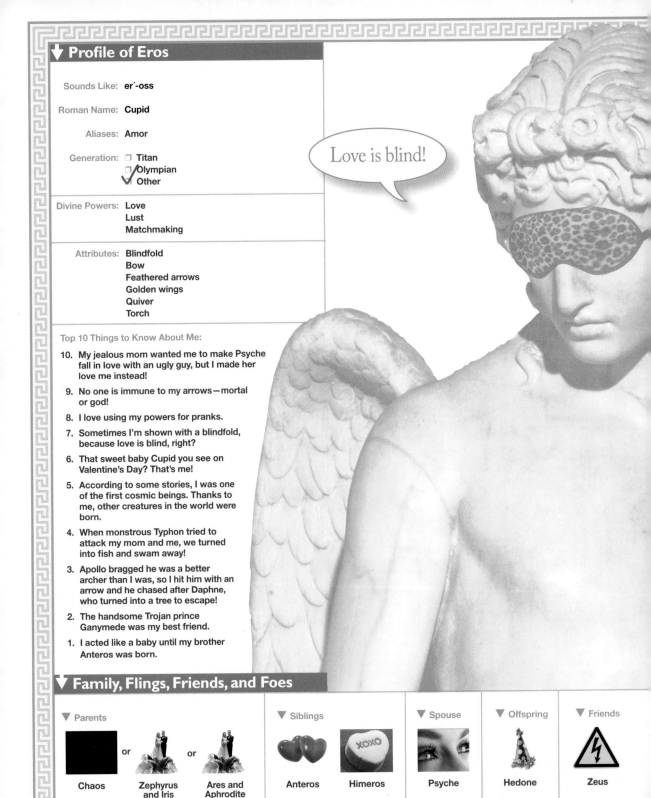

Profile of Eros

Sounds Like: er´-oss

Roman Name: Cupid

Aliases: Amor

Generation:
- ☐ Titan
- ☐ Olympian
- ☑ Other

Divine Powers: Love
Lust
Matchmaking

Attributes: Blindfold
Bow
Feathered arrows
Golden wings
Quiver
Torch

Love is blind!

Top 10 Things to Know About Me:

10. My jealous mom wanted me to make Psyche fall in love with an ugly guy, but I made her love me instead!

9. No one is immune to my arrows—mortal or god!

8. I love using my powers for pranks.

7. Sometimes I'm shown with a blindfold, because love is blind, right?

6. That sweet baby Cupid you see on Valentine's Day? That's me!

5. According to some stories, I was one of the first cosmic beings. Thanks to me, other creatures in the world were born.

4. When monstrous Typhon tried to attack my mom and me, we turned into fish and swam away!

3. Apollo bragged he was a better archer than I was, so I hit him with an arrow and he chased after Daphne, who turned into a tree to escape!

2. The handsome Trojan prince Ganymede was my best friend.

1. I acted like a baby until my brother Anteros was born.

Family, Flings, Friends, and Foes

▼ Parents

Chaos or Zephyrus and Iris or Ares and Aphrodite

▼ Siblings

Anteros Himeros

▼ Spouse

Psyche

▼ Offspring

Hedone

▼ Friends

Zeus

48

EROS
TARGET PRACTICE

Zing! Whoa, sorry Psyche! I didn't mean to hit you. I'm just practicing my aim, shooting my gold love arrows. Hey, don't look at me, girl—you know the rules. Love is blind! Yo! There's Apollo. *Zing*! Got you good with the gold, buddy. Now watch this. Hey, Daphne! *Zing*! That was a lead arrow—wait until you see what happens next! *Zing*!

REALITY CHECK

Eros (Roman Cupid), in the form of a winged cherub with a bow and arrow, is a familiar symbol on Valentine's Day. The actual St. Valentine, for whom the holiday is named, is the patron saint of engaged couples, happy marriages, and love.

Want to know more? Go to: http://www.history.com/minisites/valentine/

Daphne

Apollo

▼ Foes

Ganymede

Apollo

Daphne

EROS

"All you need is love ..."

MYTHLOPEDIA

Ερως

IT'S GREEK TO ME

In the earliest myths, Eros (love) was said to be responsible for inspiring the creation of earth, sky, sun, and moon. Later myths describe him as a handsome winged youth who flew about shooting love arrows at gods and mortals.

Eros was here!

FIRST GOD?

It all started with Eros—maybe.

Eros, the god of love, had a mysterious beginning. Some say Eros was the very first being, born out of the void known as **Chaos**. After all, nothing could be born without love! Eros then single-handedly inspired the creation of the earth, sky, sun, and moon, setting the entire universe in motion. Another version of the story explains that from Chaos there emerged a huge egg that contained the sky (Uranus), the earth (Gaea), and love (Eros). After that, Eros was imagined to be a violent **personification** of destructive lust and love. Still other stories suggest that Eros's parents were Iris, goddess of the rainbow, and Zephyrus, god of the warm west wind. What a romantic parentage for the god of love! In later stories, Eros was a youthful, mischievous god, often represented as a baby, who was born to Aphrodite, goddess of love, and her war-loving boyfriend Ares.

REALITY CHECK

Paging Dr. Freud! Austrian psychiatrist Sigmund Freud used Eros's name to refer to the positive life force that drives humankind.

Will you be my valentine?

I ♥ YOU

Sigmund Freud

LOVE + SOUL

Eros falls for Psyche and learns that love hurts.

Eros

Apollo

Daphne

Io

Semele

In one story, Eros's mom, Aphrodite, was jealous of the **mortal** Psyche, who was thought to be even more beautiful than Aphrodite. Aphrodite sent Eros to punish Psyche by making her fall in love with an ugly man. Instead, Eros fell in love with Psyche! He took her to his enchanted palace, where Psyche was treated like a goddess. But there was one condition: Psyche was not allowed to look at Eros.

Psyche was so happy that she invited her sisters to visit. Her envious sisters planted seeds of doubt in her mind, hinting that Eros might not be as great as he seemed. Psyche had to know the truth, so she snuck a peek at Eros while he slept. When she accidentally woke Eros, he fled, scolding Psyche for breaking her promise. Desperate to win Eros back, Psyche became one of Aphrodite's attendants. Eros, who still loved Psyche, persuaded Zeus to intervene. Zeus convinced Aphrodite to be kinder to Psyche. Then Zeus made Psyche immortal and allowed her to marry Eros.

REALITY CHECK

Psyche's name means "soul" so her union with Eros is literally the union of "love" and "soul."

BULL'S-EYE!

Eros creates one messy love affair after another.

Eros used his arrows to cause some love affairs that ended in tragedy. Perhaps that's one reason why he is often portrayed as an immature baby or described as irresponsible and dangerous. For example, to get even with the god Apollo for mocking his archery skills, Eros made him fall in love with the **nymph** Daphne, who preferred to turn into a tree rather than accept Apollo's love. Many of Zeus's ill-fated relationships began with Eros's arrows, like his union with Semele (she died) and his romance with Io (she was turned into a cow). Even Eros's own mother, Aphrodite, wasn't safe from his arrows—some stories say that's how she fell in love with both Ares and the handsome mortal Adonis!

REALITY CHECK

Handmade Valentine cards have been exchanged in the United States since the early 1700s. Today, about one billion Valentines are exchanged each year.

Roses are red.
My arrow has a point.
Here's hoping my aim
Won't disappoint!
-Eros

▼ Profile of Hades

Sounds Like: **hayʹ-deez**

Roman Name: **Pluto**

Aliases: **Pluton, Dis, Clymenus, Eubuleus, Polydegmon, Orcus, the Rich One**

Generation: ☐ Titan
☑ **Olympian**
☐ Other

I could use a vacation.

Divine Powers: **Underworld**
Ruler of the dead
Underground wealth

Attributes:

Asphodel	**Immortal black cattle**
Black sheep	**Mint**
Cerberus	**Narcissus**
Cypress	**Pomegranate**
Ebony throne	**Screech owl**
Golden chariot	**Secular games**
Golden keys	**Staff**
Helmet of invisibility	**White poplar**

Top 10 Things to Know About Me:

10. I'm the god of the Underworld, the ruler of the dead, and the god of death.

9. My brothers Zeus, Poseidon, and I drew lots to decide who'd rule what—and that's how I became the king of the Underworld.

8. You could call me the original "he who must not be named."

7. I kidnapped Persephone to be my wife, causing a terrible famine around the world.

6. I didn't have any biological kids since the god of the dead can't create life.

5. Living underground with dead people makes me kind of gloomy.

4. I'm not evil, but if anyone tries to cheat death, I fly into a rage!

3. My flings with Minthe and Leuce ended badly for them, thanks to my wife, Persephone.

2. Nobody bothers praying to me because I never answer prayers.

1. I'm called "the Rich One" because I have so much.

▼ Family, Flings, Friends, and Foes

▼ Parents

▼ Siblings

▼ Spouse

▼ Flings

Cronus and Rhea

Zeus

Poseidon

Hestia

Hera

Demeter

Persephone

Minthe

Leuce

HADES

I SEE DEAD PEOPLE

Welcome to the House of Hades, souls of the dead! I'll be your host this evening. Did I say this evening? I meant for eternity! If you've been brave and heroic, you'll enjoy your afterlife in the Elysian Fields. If you're immortal, it's off to Tartarus for you. And if you've been good *and* bad, you'll go to Erebus, a gloomy place where no one smiles. Hey, cheer up! It's only forever! Oh—and watch out for my dog!

Grrrrr!

Cerberus

▼ Friends

Thanatos

Orpheus

Eurydice

▼ Foes

Asclepius

Sisyphus

Demeter

▼ Pets

Cerberus

HADES

"Feel the burn!"

Άδης

"That's just my luck … I can't believe I picked the short stick!"

IT'S GREEK TO ME

In the religion of ancient Greece, the dead were cremated and their souls went to the Underworld (the "House of Hades"). Also known as the death realm, this region was ruled by the god Hades and his queen, Persephone.

Hello from Hades.

UNLUCKY LOTS

Hades loses out—but gains the entire Underworld.

After the gods Zeus, Poseidon, and Hades defeated the Titans in the Titanomachy, they controlled the whole universe—earth, sky, sea, and **Underworld**. But how would these three powerful gods decide who would rule each part? The only fair way, Zeus decided, was to draw **lots**. Each brother took a chance and hoped for the best part to rule. The result? All three gods were to rule the earth. Zeus's pick also gave him the sky, and Poseidon's gave him the sea. Hades ended up with the third portion—the Underworld, or death realm. At first Hades wasn't happy about his pick.

Underworld

But once Zeus explained that every dead soul would be one of his subjects, and that all the underground wealth would be his, Hades realized that the Underworld was a fine area to rule. And the Underworld certainly seemed to be a good fit for Hades' gloomy personality.

Persephone
Hades

PERSEPHONE, QUEEN OF THE DEAD

Even the god of the dead
needs a mate.

As god of the Underworld, Hades was surrounded by thousands of dead souls and many faithful assistants, but he longed for female companionship. Zeus decided that Persephone, his daughter with Demeter (the goddess of crops, especially grain), would make a fine match for Hades. So Hades kidnapped Persephone and dragged her down to the Underworld, where he made her his queen.

Demeter was heartbroken at the loss of her daughter and searched for her everywhere. While searching, she neglected the crops, so the harvest was ruined and people starved. Zeus had to do something. He insisted that Hades return Persephone to her mother—if, and only if, Persephone had not eaten anything in the Underworld. Because Hades did not want Persephone to return to earth, he had deliberately given her a ripe pomegranate and she had eaten a few of its seeds. Zeus agreed to a compromise: Persephone would spend four months of the year with Hades in the Underworld, and the other eight months with Demeter on earth. This story illustrates the changing seasons. When Persephone is with her mother, crops flourish. When she is with Hades, crops wither and die.

Pomegranate seeds, mmm!

Mint

LOVE IS DEAD

Most of Hades' romantic entanglements end badly— for the ladies!

Hades' dramatic kidnapping of his future queen, Persephone, didn't keep him from continuing to look for love in all the wrong places. But Hades now had to hide his romances from his jealous bride, who was fiercely possessive of her husband.

In one sad story, Hades fell in love with the **nymph** Minthe. When Minthe made the mistake of bragging that Hades loved her more than he loved Persephone, the queen of the Underworld trampled Minthe into the dirt! From Minthe's remains grew the herb we know as mint. In another tale, Hades loved a nymph named Leuce. When Persephone learned of their romance, she transformed Leuce into a white poplar tree—a tree that then became sacred to Hades.

"I can't help it if I'm poplar ... I mean *popular*!"

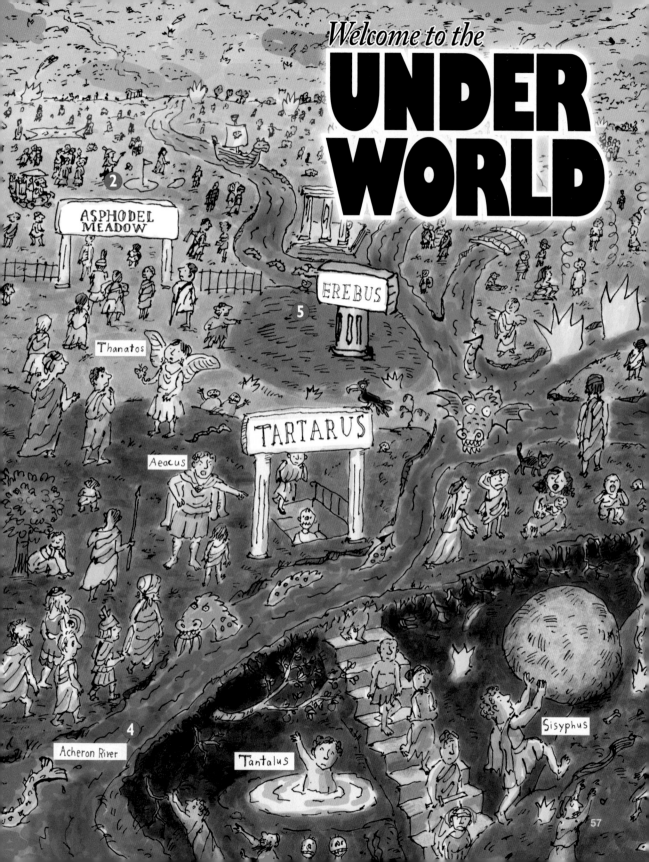

"On behalf of our staff, welcome to the House of Hades. We'll do our best to make your stay unforgettable—after all, you're our guest forever!"

MEET THE STAFF OF THE UNDER WORLD

CHARON ▶
Cap'n Charon welcomes your soul aboard his ferry for a one-way trip across the River Styx, from the land of the living to the realm of the dead. Charon has successfully transported souls to the House of Hades forever.

◀ HERMES
When you're dead, put your soul in the capable hands of Hermes, the fleet-footed messenger of the Olympians and Hades' trusted herald.

◀ THE JUDGES
In the Underworld, we pay careful attention to all of your deeds on Earth. Our judges, Aeacus and his brothers Rhadamanthus and Minos, will select the best place for you to spend eternity.

CERBERUS ▲
Round-the-clock security is provided by our highly trained watchdog, Cerberus. Forget something at home? Nobody's leaving on Cerberus's watch. Don't give it another thought! He may look vicious but a lullaby makes him sleep like a puppy.

THANATOS ▲
With his gentle touch, Thanatos, the personification of death, will send you into a peaceful—and permanent—sleep. His pet butterfly will show your soul how to fly. CAUTION: If you wake up in the morning, YOU'RE NOT DEAD!

PLACES TO VISIT

❶ ELYSIAN FIELDS

Spend eternity with the VIPs in Elysian Fields (Elysium to the locals), a land of wonder, bliss, and contentment. This lovely plain sits high on the banks of the River Oceanus at the western end of the earth. That's right … where the sun never sets!

❷ ASPHODEL MEADOW

It feels like home. You'll recognize a lot of our guests here in Asphodel Meadow, a region of neutral existence for those who spent their lives on earth doing the best they could, most of the time. Hey—everybody makes mistakes! We're filling up fast, so make your reservations early.

❸ RIVER STYX

Cruise the River Styx, the "Boundary to the Underworld." Our ferry captain Charon awaits to ensure your safe crossing into Hades. Before you step aboard, why not stop by the scenic overlook and take a final oath beside the river? Vows spoken in the name of Styx can never be broken.

❹ ACHERON RIVER

You'll say "woe is me" when you reach the murky and foul Acheron River. Ferry captain Charon will be glad to guide your soul to the Underworld— provided you brought correct change. Still living? You'll need to present a golden bough from the Cumaean Sibyl.

❺ EREBUS

As part of our ongoing effort to improve the Underworld experience, we've added the new Erebus "All Night, All the Time" system. Erebus provides the perpetual mysterious darkness that surrounds the death realm, through which all souls pass on their journey to the Underworld.

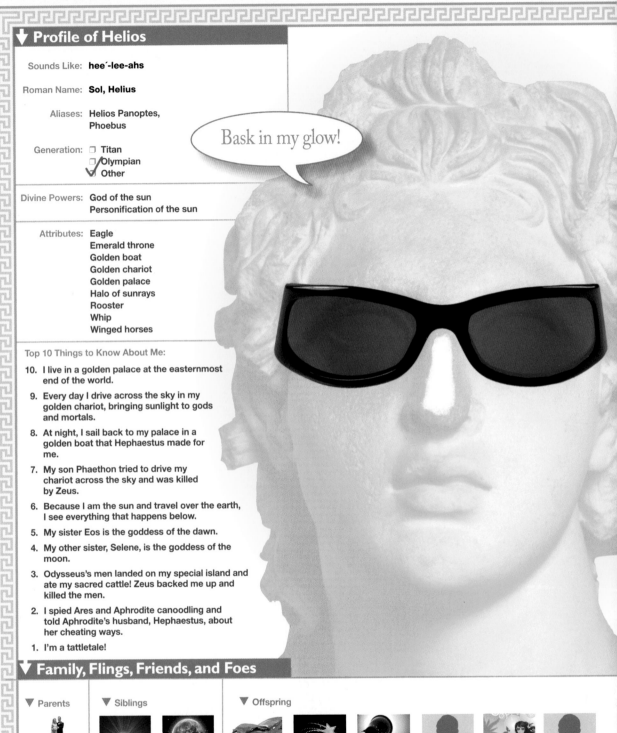

▼ Profile of Helios

Sounds Like: **hee´-lee-ahs**

Roman Name: **Sol, Helius**

Aliases: **Helios Panoptes, Phoebus**

Generation: ☐ Titan
☐ Olympian
☑ Other

Bask in my glow!

Divine Powers: **God of the sun**
Personification of the sun

Attributes: **Eagle**
Emerald throne
Golden boat
Golden chariot
Golden palace
Halo of sunrays
Rooster
Whip
Winged horses

Top 10 Things to Know About Me:

10. I live in a golden palace at the easternmost end of the world.

9. Every day I drive across the sky in my golden chariot, bringing sunlight to gods and mortals.

8. At night, I sail back to my palace in a golden boat that Hephaestus made for me.

7. My son Phaethon tried to drive my chariot across the sky and was killed by Zeus.

6. Because I am the sun and travel over the earth, I see everything that happens below.

5. My sister Eos is the goddess of the dawn.

4. My other sister, Selene, is the goddess of the moon.

3. Odysseus's men landed on my special island and ate my sacred cattle! Zeus backed me up and killed the men.

2. I spied Ares and Aphrodite canoodling and told Aphrodite's husband, Hephaestus, about her cheating ways.

1. I'm a tattletale!

▼ Family, Flings, Friends, and Foes

▼ Parents

Hyperion and Theia

▼ Siblings

Eos

Selene

▼ Offspring

Phaethon

Circe

Lampetia

Aietes

The Heliades

Phaethusa

HELIOS

CRUISIN' WITH THE SUN GOD

Ready to catch some rays? Then hop in for a spin with the sun! I'm dazzling and dashing in my golden chariot, and with my horses of fire leading the way, you can ride across the sky in total luxury. Then we'll take an evening river-cruise home. See all, know all (just spy on your friends and family, like I do), as we fly above the earth. Like gold? Then you'll like what I've got. Sunblock *highly* recommended.

REALITY CHECK

During World War II, the U.S. Navy named a repair ship the USS *Helios* after the sun god himself.

> You scorched me, dude.

▼ **Flings**

Merope

Clymene

▼ **Friends**

Demeter

Hephaestus

Apollo

▼ **Foes**

Odysseus

Zeus

Hades

Ares

HELIOS

"Here comes the sun."

MYTHLOPEDIA

Ηλιος

IT'S GREEK TO ME

When Zeus divided earthly realms among the gods, Helios was left out. So he requested the island of Rhodes and became its divine **patron**. High above the harbor, the citizens erected a bronze statue of Helios wearing a sun-ray crown and looking out to sea. Built between 292–280 BCE, the statue, known as the Colossus of Rhodes, became one of the Seven Wonders of the World. It fell in an earthquake around 220 BCE.

Colossus of Rhodes

HIP TO BE HELIOS

Helios shines in everything he does.

Helios, as dazzling as the sun he carried across the sky each day, lived in total luxury befitting his golden status. Not surprisingly, Helios's world was rich with gold. His blond head was crowned with a shining **aureole** made of the sun's rays, and light seemed to pour from his eyes. His golden **chariot** was drawn by winged horses of fire. His palace, located at the easternmost edge of the world, was made of solid gold. Each morning, after his sister Eos, goddess of the dawn, made her trip across the sky, Helios raced across the sky in his golden chariot, carrying the sun along with him. In the evening, he arrived at the westernmost part of the world as the sun set in the west. Then, overnight, he sailed back to his palace in a golden boat. Helios had an important job, and he did it in style.

Here comes the sun god!

"Hey, Dad, can I borrow the chariot today?"

PHAETHON'S JOYRIDE

Helios's son is no match for the sun.

Phaethon

Helios's son Phaethon wanted to drive his dad's sparkling golden chariot—and the sun—across the sky. So Phaethon asked Helios for a favor, without saying what it was. Helios agreed, and swore a vow, or promise. Then Phaethon told Helios that he wanted to drive his chariot.

Helios immediately regretted his vow. He knew that Phaethon was too young and weak to control the powerful horses that led the chariot. With a heavy heart, he handed the reins to his son. Phaethon cracked his father's whip and the chariot sped into the sky. But just as

Helios had predicted, Phaethon was unable to control the chariot. It zoomed so far into space that the earth grew cold and frozen; then it **careened** so close to the planet that the sun scorched huge deserts into the land. Gaea complained to Zeus, who knew of only one way to solve the problem. He hit Phaethon with one of his thunderbolts, instantly killing the boy. Phaethon, the horses, the chariot, and even the sun crashed to the earth, creating the desert area we now know as the Sahara.

HOT!

BURGER BUMMER

Odysseus's men pay for a snack of sacred cows—with their lives!

Helios kept his sacred herd of red cattle on the island of Thrinacia. There his daughters Phaethusa and Lampetia spent their days and nights caring for the special beasts.

After fighting in the Trojan War, the hero Odysseus and his men faced a long and perilous voyage home. Along the way, they stopped on Thrinacia, and much to Odysseus's shock and shame, his men slaughtered and ate some of Helios's sacred cattle—despite Odysseus's warnings not to do such a foolish thing! Phaethusa and Lampetia told their father about the terrible offense. Helios complained to Zeus, who responded by sinking Odysseus's ship and killing all the men aboard it—except for Odysseus, who had been wise enough to avoid offending the sun god.

Don't look at me like that. I'm sacred!

Profile of Hephaestus

Sounds Like: huh-fes´-tuhs

Roman Name: Vulcan

Aliases: Mulciber

Generation:
☐ Titan
☑ Olympian
☐ Other

Divine Powers: Fire
Forges
Handicrafts
Metalworking
Volcanoes

Attributes: Anvil
Ax
Blacksmith's fire
Donkey
Golden crutches
Hammer
Island of Lemnos
Tongs

Anything for you, dear!

Top 10 Things to Know About Me:

10. My mom, Hera, was so ashamed of my ugliness that she threw me out of Olympus—literally!

9. My fall crushed my legs and left me with a limp.

8. I'm generally a friendly guy.

7. After Hera saw how talented I was (especially at making bling) she begged me to come home.

6. Zeus gave me Aphrodite as my wife, but he couldn't give me her heart.

5. When Zeus had a killer headache, I cracked his head open with an ax. Out popped the goddess Athena, fully formed!

4. I got even with Hera by creating a throne that trapped her when she sat down.

3. I set a trap for my cheating wife, Aphrodite, and caught her with my half brother, Ares!

2. I created the first woman, Pandora, out of clay. Zeus used her to punish men.

1. I stayed in my underground workshop rather than hang out on Olympus with deities who made fun of me.

▼ Family, Flings, Friends, and Foes

▼ Parents	▼ Siblings		▼ Spouse	▼ Offspring		▼ Flings	
Zeus and Hera	Ares	Eileithyia	Aphrodite	Erichthonius	The Kabeiroi	Charis	Aglaia

HEPHAESTUS

BEAUTY IS SKIN DEEP

Zeus, slow down—it's hard to keep up with my feet on backward. About your order that I marry Aphrodite—listen, I appreciate it. She's gorgeous! Everyone loves her! But I'm, well, not so easy on the eyes with all my, er, unwanted hair, my fat neck, and my problem skin. All that's beautiful about me are the things I make. Wouldn't she be happier with someone … more handsome? No, I'm not second-guessing you! Put away that thunderbolt—marrying her would be my pleasure!

> Honey, I need some new bling.

Aphrodite

▼ Friends

Dionysus **Thetis** **Eurynome**

▼ Foes

Hera **Ares**

HEPHAESTUS

"Looks aren't everything."

MYTH LOPEDIA

Ηφαιστος

"My own mother couldn't stand the sight of me!"

I won't forget this, Mom!

IT'S GREEK TO ME

The Roman counterpart to Hephaestus is Vulcan, the god of volcanic fire and the **patron** of arts and crafts (especially metalworking) associated with fire. His marriage to Venus, the Roman goddess of love, was symbolic of the union of artistic craft with grace and beauty.

MOMMY DEAREST

Hera is not exactly Mother of the Year.

Zeus's wife, Hera, was known for seeking revenge, but her treatment of her son Hephaestus was among the worst of her cruel acts. She found her baby so repulsive that she threw him out of Olympus! Hephaestus fell for an entire week before crashing into the sea.

According to another story, Hephaestus had no father because Hera wanted to get even with Zeus for producing Athena without her, so she decided to have a child by herself, too. But when she saw Hephaestus, she was so ashamed of his ugliness that she decided to eliminate the evidence. No matter what her reasons, Hera was clearly a terrible mother. But Hephaestus got his revenge in the end. After he grew up and became a master craftsman, he designed a gorgeous golden throne for his mother. When she sat on it, the throne held her prisoner—and Hephaestus refused to free her until his demands were met!

Ha-ha! You're trapped now!

Hera

Hephaestus

Oceanid

NICE NYMPHS

Ocean nymphs raise Hephaestus right.

Hephaestus was a god from the moment he was born—but even a god can find himself in a dangerous situation. That is exactly what happened when Hera threw the newborn Hephaestus off Mount Olympus.

Hephaestus's fate might have been entirely different had it not been for two loving Oceanids named Thetis and Eurynome. Oceanids, or water **nymphs**, were daughters of Oceanus and there were over 4,000 of them. For nine years, Thetis and Eurynome kept Hephaestus on the island of Lemnos, safe from Hera's vengeful wrath. There he grew to adulthood and honed his skills as a master craftsman.

AN OPENING ON OLYMPUS

Hera has a change of heart about kicking Hephaestus off the Mount.

Handy Hephaestus shared his marvelous creations with anyone who had shown him kindness. Eurynome and Thetis soon had enough stunning jewelry made of precious metals and sparkling jewels to adorn an entire **pantheon** of goddesses. When Hera saw the bling, she knew at once that only a god with extraordinary skill could have made it. She suspected that it was the work of the son she'd disowned.

Hera began to regret her cruel actions, if for no other reason than her son might now make her proud. And she wanted some of that gorgeous jewelry, too. But when she sweetly invited Hephaestus to take his rightful place on Mount Olympus, he refused! Zeus agreed that a god as skilled as Hephaestus belonged on Olympus, so he sent Dionysus to bring him back. Hephaestus reluctantly agreed to take his place on Olympus for official business—but he still preferred to spend time in his underground workshop on the island of Lemnos.

PANDORA'S JAR (YES, JAR!)

Hephaestus makes the first woman, and she makes a BIG boo-boo.

Pandora (meaning "all gifted") was the first woman on earth. She was created out of clay by Hephaestus, on orders from Zeus, as punishment for all men after Prometheus defied the gods and stole fire from the heavens to give to **mortals**. The gods gave Pandora the gifts of beauty and charm, along with a powerful curiosity. Zeus gave her a gift, too: a magic jar (sometimes called Pandora's box). Zeus warned Pandora not to open it but she couldn't resist. Overcome with curiosity, she opened the lid. Out poured all the troubles and diseases the world has ever known. By the time she closed the lid, only hope remained in the jar.

Trouble!

Pandora

FATHER OF INVENTION

Whatever you want, Hephaestus can make it!

Back on Mount Olympus, Hephaestus began to create powerful objects for the gods and goddesses—right after he got revenge against Hera with the golden throne that imprisoned her. He designed and built many of the Olympians' regal palaces and thrones. He also created Aphrodite's belt of irresistibility—when she wore it, she became even more desirable to everyone she met. He made a cursed necklace and robe as a wedding gift for Harmonia, the goddess of harmony, which gave the wearer the ability to cause strife and unhappiness; the dangerous ensemble caused many deaths. Hephaestus crafted the hero Achilles' indestructible armor and a nearly invisible net that Hephaestus used to ensnare Ares and Aphrodite. Hephaestus made the sun god Helios's boat and **chariot**. For his own use, Hephaestus invented two golden handmaidens to help him move from place to place— perhaps the world's first robots!

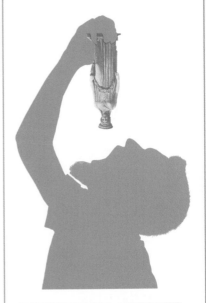

You are so handsome! We love you. You are so handsome…

Heph's helpers

A WORRIED FATHER

Zeus swallows his troubles.

Before Hephaestus was born, Zeus was married to a wise goddess named Metis. When the couple was expecting their first baby, it was prophesied that Metis would give birth to a child who would be more powerful than its father. Zeus started to worry. He believed that the only solution to this dilemma would be to keep Metis from giving birth to the child. So, like his own father Cronus had done with his children, Zeus swallowed Metis whole! Metis didn't die, but instead gave Zeus advice from within.

AX MAN

Hephaestus cures Zeus's splitting headache—and out pops a surprise!

Many years after he swallowed Metis, Zeus suffered with a terrible headache. Trying to be helpful, Hephaestus grabbed his ax and, using all his strength, struck Zeus on the head. From the gash in Zeus's head sprang the fully grown goddess Athena! Athena had all of her mother Metis's wisdom, but because she had been born only from her father, the **prophecy** that had so worried Zeus was avoided.

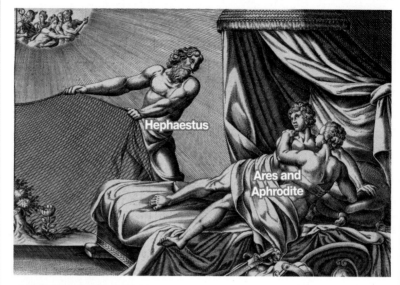

Hephaestus

Ares and Aphrodite

OPPOSITES DON'T ATTRACT

This arranged marriage was doomed from day one.

How did the only ugly god on Olympus (Hephaestus) end up married to the most beautiful and desirable goddess (Aphrodite)? Easy answer: Zeus! The mighty god ordered this arranged marriage to take place and not even Aphrodite could disobey his divine word. Not surprisingly, the match was doomed from the start. Aphrodite knew that she had to marry Hephaestus, but Zeus could not force her to be faithful to him. She soon struck up a romance with Ares, the god of war. When Helios spied them together, he tattled to Hephaestus. Wanting to see the cheating pair with his own eyes, Hephaestus made a net of gold chains so thin that they were nearly invisible. When Ares and Aphrodite snuck off together, the trap was sprung, and they were caught in the net. Hephaestus asked all the gods to come judge his unfaithful wife. But to his dismay, they found the situation hilarious. Hephaestus eventually freed Ares and Aphrodite from the net.

> "Aphrodite may be a dish, but she's no picnic."

My head is killing me.

Hephaestus

Zeus

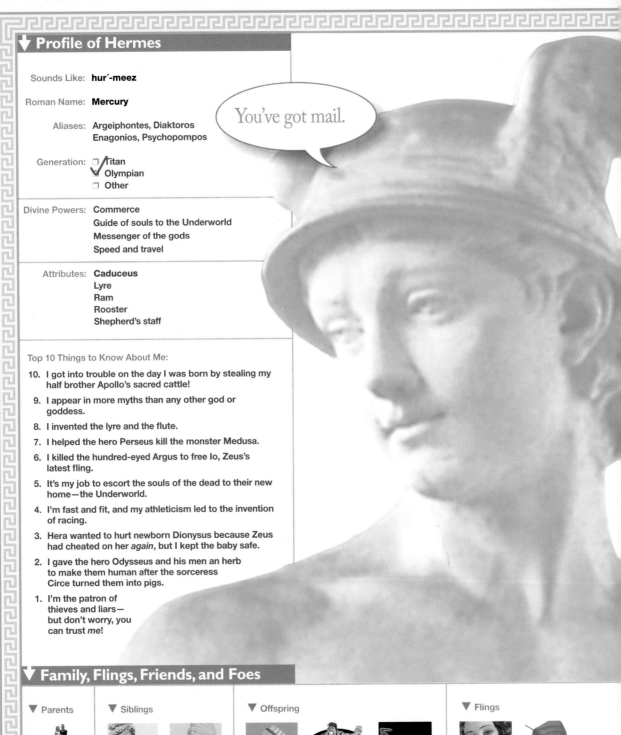

▼ Profile of Hermes

Sounds Like: hur´-meez

Roman Name: Mercury

Aliases: Argeiphontes, Diaktoros
Enagonios, Psychopompos

Generation: ☐ Titan
☑ Olympian
☐ Other

You've got mail.

Divine Powers: Commerce
Guide of souls to the Underworld
Messenger of the gods
Speed and travel

Attributes: **Caduceus**
Lyre
Ram
Rooster
Shepherd's staff

Top 10 Things to Know About Me:

10. I got into trouble on the day I was born by stealing my half brother Apollo's sacred cattle!

9. I appear in more myths than any other god or goddess.

8. I invented the lyre and the flute.

7. I helped the hero Perseus kill the monster Medusa.

6. I killed the hundred-eyed Argus to free Io, Zeus's latest fling.

5. It's my job to escort the souls of the dead to their new home—the Underworld.

4. I'm fast and fit, and my athleticism led to the invention of racing.

3. Hera wanted to hurt newborn Dionysus because Zeus had cheated on her *again*, but I kept the baby safe.

2. I gave the hero Odysseus and his men an herb to make them human after the sorceress Circe turned them into pigs.

1. I'm the patron of thieves and liars— but don't worry, you can trust *me*!

▼ Family, Flings, Friends, and Foes

▼ Parents

Zeus and Maia

▼ Siblings

Apollo

Artemis

▼ Offspring

Pan

Autolycus

Hermaphroditus

▼ Flings

Aphrodite

Dryope

HERMES
HAVE I GOT A DEAL FOR YOU!

Psssst. Check it out. You looking for a custom-made lyre? How about this sweet flute? It fell right off the back of a chariot. What about this cow from Apollo's herd? I've had it since I was a baby. It's guaranteed 100 percent sacred beef. You won't find a better deal anywhere. What? You don't want to annoy the god of prophecy? I hear you, friend. Can I interest you in these winged sandals? They're just like mine, and mine have traveled the world *and* the Underworld.

Mercury

Hermes' sandals

▼ Friends

Crocus

Penelope

Odysseus

Hera

Perseus

▼ Foes

Argus

Medusa

HERMES

"I was the first multitasker."

MYTH LOPEDIA

Ερμης

"What's a myth without me? Two words: BO-RING!"

IT'S GREEK TO ME

Hermes was originally an ancient Arcadian god of cattle, sheep, and fertility. Arcadia is a mountainous area in the center of the Greek Peloponnesus, or southernmost mainland Greece.

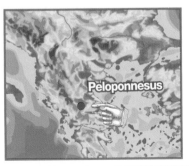

Peloponnesus

ZIP, ZIP, ZOOM!

Hermes makes a dashing messenger.

Hermes was a god with many talents and many responsibilities. He was perhaps most famous for his winged sandals. And no wonder: With those sandals on his feet, Hermes could move incredibly fast. His speed was part of the reason for one of Hermes' very important jobs: messenger, or **herald**, of almighty Zeus. In this role, Hermes was responsible for delivering Zeus's messages to **mortals** and other gods, often bringing a reply to Zeus in return. When Hermes had to deliver news that Zeus didn't want to hear, his speed came in handy—helping him leap out of the way of flying thunderbolts! With his reputation for speed

and agility, it's no surprise that Hermes was imagined as a youthful, athletic, and muscular god, with a special interest in the sport of gymnastics.

"Wanna race? You lose!"

Mount Olympus Police
SPEEDING TICKET

NAME: Hermes   DATE: Eternity

LOCATION: Mount Olympus

OFFENSE: Racing 50 mph over the speed limit

OFFICER'S NOTES: Suspect noted to be racing around a mountain pass marked "Treacherous" and "Caution. Slow." Suspect detained for questioning and possible ticketing. Suspect very remorseful; promised to never speed again. Suspect maintained a cheerful attitude and complimented my uniform.

SIGNED:

3 8 0 2 2 8 7

3802287

Such a smart little boy, that Hermes!

SNEAKY AND SLY

A baby has a busy day.

Hermes was born early one morning in a cave. While his exhausted mother, Maia, rested, the infant Hermes crawled out of his cradle and zoomed off down the road. Eventually he came to his half brother Apollo's herd of sacred cattle—and promptly stole some of them! The sly tot covered his tracks by walking away backward (and somehow convincing the cows to walk backward, too).

On the way home, young Hermes captured and killed a tortoise, making the world's first **lyre** out of its shell. He then hid the stolen cattle and crawled back into his cradle, before Maia even awoke. When Apollo discovered who had stolen his cattle, he demanded that Hermes return them. Hermes tried to defend himself by saying that he was just a baby. But

Zeus had been watching the whole episode and ordered Hermes to return the cattle to Apollo. Hermes started playing a song on the lyre he had invented. Apollo was so delighted by the new instrument that he offered to let Hermes keep the cattle in exchange for the lyre. Now Apollo had a new favorite instrument— and Hermes was well on his way to establishing himself as a sneaky and sly god.

REALITY CHECK

The lyre is a stringed instrument. It consists of a resonance box or bowl with strings suspended from the base to a crossbar supported by two arms parallel to its surface. The earliest lyres date to about 3000 BCE.

Want to know more? Go to:
http://www.lyre-of-ur.com

lyre

Hermes

dead soul

"All aboard the soul train!"

SOUL GUIDE

Hermes guides the souls of the dead to the Underworld.

One of Hermes' most mysterious duties was as a conductor of the souls of the dead to the **Underworld**. Hermes was chosen to be a herald of Hades, perhaps because he was a favorite of Zeus, and Zeus knew that he could be trusted with this important job. With his golden **caduceus**, Hermes attracted the souls to him, then led them in a large group to the banks of the River Styx. He then turned the souls over to Charon, who ferried them across the river to the House of Hades for a small fee.

"I'm on a roll!"

Hermes

ALSO STARRING HERMES (AS HIMSELF)

Zeus's right-hand man appears in many myths.

Because of his role as Zeus's **herald**, or messenger, Hermes makes appearances in many well-known myths. It was Hermes who was sent to the **Underworld** to bring Persephone, queen of the Underworld, back to her mother, Demeter. For the weddings of Zeus and Hera, and Eros and Psyche, Hermes delivered invitations to all the **deities**. Zeus also sent Hermes to try to force Prometheus to reveal a secret **prophecy** about Zeus's downfall, which only he knew. And when Zeus got tired of Poseidon wrathfully flooding cities, he sent Hermes to deliver his message to the god of the sea. Hermes delivered a message to Calypso telling her to free the hero Odysseus. And Hermes also brought the first **mortal** woman, Pandora, to mortal men after her creation by Hephaestus.

REALITY CHECK

The first Goodyear blimp was built in 1925. During World War II, blimps were used for surveillance. Today, Goodyear describes them as "aerial ambassadors" and they are often seen at major sporting events. And guess whose winged sandals are on the side of every blimp? Right: Hermes'!

Want to know more? Go to: http://www.goodyearblimp.com

INVENTIVE MINDS

Clever Hermes makes good use of his mind.

Renowned for his cleverness as well as for his quick wit, Hermes' inventions show he was a god of many talents. In addition to the **lyre**, which he invented when he was one day old, Hermes also invented the flute and possibly the **panpipe**, although many stories attribute their creation to Pan. Hermes also invented sports such as racing and wrestling. He invented the concept of sacrifices as a part of divine worship by sacrificing some of Apollo's cattle to the Olympian gods. Impressed yet? There's more. He also might have been responsible for the invention of numbers and the alphabet!

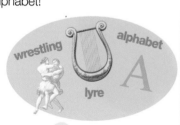

Hermes'
inventions

ATTACK ON ARGUS

Hermes kills the jailer of Zeus's love, Io.

One of Zeus's many loves was the beautiful maiden Io, a priestess of Zeus's wife, Hera. Hera responded by turning Io into a white cow. Then she commanded the hundred-eyed giant Argus to guard Io so that Zeus couldn't get near her. With his many eyes, Argus was able to keep watch in every direction.

Undeterred, Zeus sent Hermes, his trusted herald, to rescue Io. Hermes lulled Argus to sleep by playing a beautiful song on his flute. While Argus slept, Hermes sliced off his head! Io was able to escape, but Hera's punishment was not over yet. She then sent a biting gadfly to torment Io, who continuously roamed the world in attempts to escape the fly. Io finally settled in Egypt, far from Zeus, where she was allowed to turn back into a woman.

REALITY CHECK

The Mercury space program (named for Hermes' fleet-footed Roman counterpart) was the earliest U.S. project to put an astronaut into space. John Glenn, Jr., flew a mission on February 20, 1962, in a Mercury spacecraft named *Friendship 7*. The spacecraft was boosted into space by an Atlas 6 rocket.

Want to know more? Go to:
www.nasa.gov/mission_pages/mercury

Is there something on my back?

Io

▼ Profile of Pan

Sounds Like: pan´

Roman Name: Faunus

Aliases: Agreus, Nomios

Generation:
- ☐ Titan
- ☐ Olympian
- ☑ Other

Divine Powers: Fertility
Forests
Hunters
Nature
Shepherds
Wildlife

Attributes: Crown of pine boughs
Goat
Lynx pelt
Mount Lycaeum
Mountain caves
Pine tree
Sheep
Shepherd's staff
Syrinx (panpipe)

I am the original party animal!

Top 10 Things to Know About Me:

10. I have the head and body of a human and the legs, horns, ears, and beard of a goat!

9. I was born with an ugly, wrinkly face and goat horns; my appearance scared my nurse so much that she ran away.

8. I invented the panpipe, thanks to the nymph Syrinx.

7. My name inspired the word *panic*. Boo!

6. Hermes is my dad.

5. The gods don't like me very much, maybe because I'm a big fan of jokes and tricks.

4. I have the gift of prophecy and my very own oracle in Arcadia.

3. I hang out with Dionysus because I love to par-tay!

2. I'm crazy for nymphs, but the feeling isn't mutual.

1. I spend a lot of time with satyrs. We half-beast, half-man creatures have to stick together!

▼ Family, Flings, Friends, and Foes

▼ Parents
Hermes and Daughter of Dryops

▼ Siblings
Hermaphroditus
Eleusis

▼ Offspring
Silenus
The Panes
Krotos
Iynx

▼ Flings
Syrinx
Pitys

PAN
WALK ON THE WILD SIDE

Tour rural Greece with me, the one and only Pan: half-goat, half-man, all fun! Visit abandoned mountain caves, deserted forests, and lonely trails and try to keep up as my hooves prance over rocky mountainsides! Play a song on the syrinx! Have a dance with Dionysus! Admire my horns in the moonlight! Meet some delightful nymphs. (Note: no guarantees about the friendliness of the nymphs.) It's an ordinary night for me— but is sure to be the best night of your life! Not for the *pan*ic-prone!

Hey, Pan! Check out the party on my page!

REALITY CHECK

There is a tiny town called Pan in Arcadia, Greece. It is right where Pan's oracle was located and the worship of Pan started.

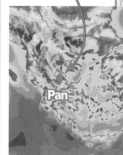
Pan

Dionysus

Echo

Omphale

▼ Friends

Dionysus

▼ Foes

Heracles

PAN

"A party! For me?"

MYTHLOPEDIA

Παν

IT'S GREEK TO ME

At ancient Greek festivals, a trio of tragedies, often featuring deeply disturbing themes, were performed. These difficult dramas were followed by a satyr play, which was usually short and very funny, to lift the spirits of everyone in the audience. Satyr plays featured a chorus of actors dressed as satyrs and masks were commonly worn during the performances.

Comedy

Tragedy

WHAT AN ANIMAL!

The satyrs live it up.

The Olympian gods resembled humans, but Pan was an entirely different kind of **deity**. His form combined human characteristics (a human face, torso, and arms) with the hairy legs, horns, and tail of a goat. Pan was not alone in his odd appearance, though. An entire class of mythological creatures, called **satyrs**, resembled him. While early artists showed satyrs as part human, part horse, over time they were shown with the same goat features as Pan. Satyrs gave in to their animal instincts without hesitation. They abandoned more civilized behavior, preferring wild parties with Dionysus and Pan.

Satyr Party

Gods gone wild!

"BOO! Scared you!"

DON'T PANIC!

Pan loves to spook everyone—even his poor mom!

From almost the moment of his birth, Pan was a strange being. He was born fully formed, with a wrinkly face, a full beard, horns, and a hairy goat's body—not exactly the soft, sweet, innocent infant his mother expected! It's no wonder that she took one look at her hideous baby and ran away. Pan's father, Hermes, took his son to Olympus, where the rest of the gods and goddesses delighted in this odd creature. This early experience with spooking others grew into a passion for Pan. He was known for hiding in the lonely, rural areas of Greece and frightening travelers by making scary noises!

REALITY CHECK

Pan's name was the inspiration for the word *panic* because that is the feeling he was said to inspire in people.

Pan

nymph

Pan

PAN AND SYRINX

A nymph's transformation leads to the invention of an instrument.

Like the satyrs, Pan often gave into his animal instincts, especially when it came to love. He constantly fell in love with woodland **nymphs**, most of whom wanted nothing to do with the grotesque creature. But that didn't stop Pan from pursuing them! He was especially infatuated with a nymph named Syrinx, who had pledged to remain pure. Pan chased Syrinx through the woods, desperate to capture her, while the nymph tried to escape. The terrified Syrinx threw herself into a river and begged for help. Sympathetic river nymphs heard her and transformed her into the hollow reeds that grew at the river's edge. Pan was so frustrated by Syrinx's escape that he cut down the hollow reeds. To his delight, Pan discovered that the wind made a beautiful noise blowing through the reeds. He tied together reeds of different lengths and the instrument called the syrinx, or **panpipe**, was born.

REALITY CHECK

The panpipe, or the pan flute (also known as a syrinx), is a popular folk instrument that dates back to ancient times. Panpipes are usually made from hollow tubes of wood, such as bamboo. You can find simple instructions on the Internet for making your own.

Want to know more? Go to:
http://pan-flute.com/history

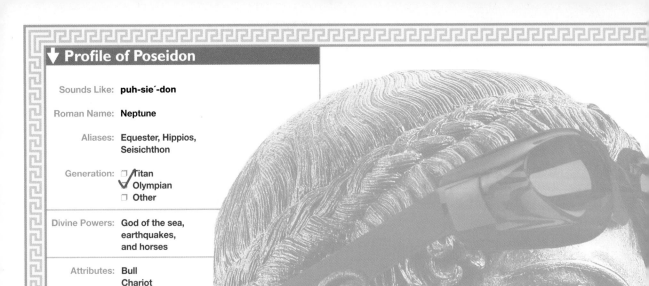

▼ Profile of Poseidon

Sounds Like: **puh-sie´-don**

Roman Name: **Neptune**

Aliases: **Equester, Hippios, Seisichthon**

Generation:
- ☐ Titan
- ☑ Olympian
- ☐ Other

Divine Powers: **God of the sea, earthquakes, and horses**

Attributes:
Bull
Chariot
Coral palace
Dolphin
Horse
Trident

Top 10 Things to Know About Me:

10. My dad, Cronus, swallowed my siblings and me (except for Zeus).

9. When I'm in a bad mood, look out for floods, earthquakes, and stormy seas!

8. After Zeus, I'm the most powerful god.

7. Athena and I competed for the patronage of the city of Athens. She won so it was named after her.

6. I was part of a plot to overthrow Zeus. He punished me with a year of hard labor!

5. Demeter turned into a mare to escape me, so I turned into a stallion and attacked her.

4. I created the first horse.

3. The king of Troy tried to cheat me so I sent a monster to attack his city!

2. I had many love affairs and lots of children.

1. Amphitrite didn't want to marry me but my pal Delphinus convinced her to. I was so grateful that I turned him into a constellation—the Dolphin.

I feel an earthquake coming on.

▼ Family, Flings, Friends, and Foes

▼ **Parents**

Cronus and Rhea

▼ **Siblings**

Zeus

Hades

Demeter

Hera

Hestia

▼ **Spouse**

Amphitrite

▼ **Offspring**

Triton

Orion

POSEIDON
ALL WASHED UP

I'm so blue today. I have to get out of this funk. Should I sink a ship? I could flood a city, but I promised Zeus I wouldn't do that anymore. Cause a drought? No, it takes too long to see the effects. Earthquakes are fun—or I could send a sea monster to land! Maybe I'll just find a new girlfriend. After all, who can resist *me*, the god of the sea?

Go to your happy place, Dad!

Pegasus

REALITY CHECK
The 2006 movie *Poseidon* is about a luxury ocean liner named SS *Poseidon* that is capsized by a 150-foot rogue wave in the middle of the ocean on New Year's Eve. What happens next? You'll have to see for yourself!

Want to know more? Go to:
www.imdb.com

Theseus

Pegasus

▼ Flings

Medusa

Demeter

Thetis

▼ Friends

Apollo

Delphinus

▼ Foes

Athena

The Trojans

"Water, water, everywhere."

Ποσειδων

"Watch out for my bad moods, dudes!"

OUCH!

Trident

IT'S GREEK TO ME

After the Olympians defeated the Titans in the ten-year battle known as the Titanomachy, Zeus and his brothers Hades and Poseidon drew **lots** to decide which realm each would rule. Zeus became the ruler of the heavens; Hades, the **Underworld**; and Poseidon, the sea. The three shared rule of the earth.

HORSING AROUND

Horses are sacred to the god of the sea.

Poseidon, the god of the sea, was also the god of horses. According to one story, Poseidon and the goddess Athena competed to win patronage of (and naming rights to) the city of Athens. Poseidon invented the horse, although other stories say he gave the city a useless fountain. However, Athena invented the olive tree, which was deemed far more useful to the city since it provided food, oil, and wood for burning. So she was awarded the patronage and Athens was named for her. In another story, Poseidon was enamored of the goddess Demeter, who transformed herself into a mare in an attempt to run away from him. Poseidon then transformed himself into a stallion to capture her. The two became the parents of the winged horse Arion. Poseidon also mated with the Gorgon Medusa before she was turned into a hideous monster. Later, when the hero Perseus killed Medusa, the winged horse Pegasus sprang from her **severed** neck.

Has anyone seen my snorkel?

> Hmm ... So many people to terrify, so little time!

Sea Monster

GROUCH OF THE SEA

Moody Poseidon sets out for revenge.

Poseidon was one of the moodiest, most spiteful gods of Olympus. When he was in a foul mood, Poseidon enjoyed churning up terrible storms at sea, or sending floods to destroy the land. When the city of Athens chose Athena over Poseidon as its **patron**, he got even by sending a flood.

After Zeus forbade him to flood any more cities, Poseidon found new ways to get revenge, such as drying up rivers and streams, causing terrible droughts, or sending earthquakes. Poseidon was even involved in a plot to overthrow Zeus—a BIG mistake. Zeus punished Poseidon by forcing him and Apollo to do hard labor, stripped of their godly powers. When the king of Troy refused to pay Poseidon and Apollo for their work, Poseidon got even by sending a sea monster to ravage the city.

Poseidon's Quick and Easy Everyday Revenge Ideas!

Floods
Fast, easy, and catastrophic!

Horrible storms
So simple—just a swirl of my trident and the seas start churning. One hour prep.

Droughts
Easy to cause, but you've got to be patient to see the results.

Sea monster attack
Send in the monsters, then watch the people scream and run!

Sinking ships
No explanation necessary!

MONSTER CONNECTION

The god of the sea has many associations with monsters.

All sea monsters were part of Poseidon's domain, and he enjoyed sending them to terrorize humans. Because he had been caught with a beauty named Medusa in one of Athena's temples, the angry goddess turned Medusa into one of the most hideous creatures of all time.

Poseidon fathered many amazing offspring, including the winged horses Pegasus and Arion. His romance with the sea **nymph** Scylla resulted in her transformation into a monster. She had been a lovely sea nymph when Poseidon fell in love with her. But his wife, Amphitrite, put a stop to their affair by turning Scylla into a hideous monster with six dog heads and twelve dog legs. Scylla spent the rest of her life attacking ships and eating sailors.

Scylla

Temple of Poseidon Attica, Greece

CITY SLICKER

The world's water isn't enough for Poseidon.

Poseidon was the god of the sea but that didn't mean he wasn't a serious force to be reckoned with on land. In fact, the sea god was very interested in what happened on land. He competed with Athena for patronage of Athens, creating the first horse (or fountain) in an attempt to win the city.

According to some stories, Poseidon struck his **trident** in the ground, creating an impressive geyser of water—but since it was salt water, it was undrinkable and useless to the people of Athens.

Poseidon was also frequently involved in battles with other gods for control of islands. He fought Hera for Argolis; when he lost, he dried up all the rivers in the area. He battled with Dionysus for the island of Naxos. He also fought against Helios for Corinth, and was granted control of the **isthmus**. Poseidon even fought against the great Zeus for the island of Aegina!

REALITY CHECK

The nation of Greece is made up of over 6,000 islands. Only 227 are inhabited.

many islands

"Islands in the ocean should be mine, all mine!"

LOVE UNDER THE SEA

Poseidon's bride-to-be can run but she can't hide forever!

Like his brother Zeus, Poseidon had many loves. His first love was a sea **nymph**, Thetis, who was one of the Nereids. Poseidon was desperate to marry her—until he heard a **prophecy** that Thetis's son would be greater than his father. Suddenly, Thetis was not such an appealing match, so Poseidon turned his attention to another Nereid, Thetis's sister Amphitrite. But Amphitrite wanted nothing to do with the moody, bullying sea god. She hid from him so well that not even the powerful Poseidon could find her. A clever dolphin named Delphinus tracked down Amphitrite, convinced her to marry Poseidon, and then brought her back to the sea god. Amphitrite and Poseidon were promptly wed, and Poseidon was so grateful to Delphinus that he placed him among the stars as the Dolphin constellation.

Poseidon

PRINCESS IN CHAINS

A hero thwarts Poseidon's plans.

Cassiopeia, the queen of Ethiopia, made the mistake of boasting that her daughter Andromeda was more beautiful than the sea nymphs known as Nereids. Poseidon was not at all pleased, so he turned to his usual tricks. He sent Cetus, a terrifying sea monster, to destroy Ethiopia. The vengeful sea god refused to call off the monster unless Andromeda was sacrificed.

To end the siege of Ethiopia, the princess was chained to a cliff by the sea and left there to die. Lucky for her, the hero Perseus rescued her and turned Cetus into stone, using the **severed** head of the Gorgon Medusa. Later, the hero and the princess were married and became king and queen of the Greek city of Tiryns.

> "Nereids, Oceanids, Naiads—who can keep them all straight?"

WIDE WORLD OF WATER

Even Poseidon needs a little help ruling the world's waters.

With a planet covered by bodies of water, including thousands of rivers, streams, lakes, ponds, and oceans, Poseidon relied on many less powerful **deities** to help him control them all. There were many sea nymphs: Nereids, the daughters of Nereus and Doris, were found in Mediterranean waters; Naiads presided over freshwater streams and springs; and Oceanids were found in salt waters like the oceans. A river god ruled each river. If a river or stream dried up, the nymph or god associated with it would die, which made Poseidon's punishment of drought all the more dangerous.

Perseus turns a sea monster to stone.

Perseus

Cetus

Andromeda

Use this handy guide to plan your visit. Just follow the numbers on the map.

POSEIDON'S WATER WORLD

① TRITON WELCOMES YOU ▶

The #1 son of Poseidon and Amphitrite wants to make your Water World visit a splashing success. Stop by and say hello (look for the merman by the entrance). Hear the blast of a conch shell? That's Triton announcing the big guy is in the house!

② OCEANUS'S RIVER RIDE ▼

Relax and enjoy the famous "Forever River Cruise" with your guide, Oceanus, one of the original founders of Water World. Circle the earth on a raft while Oceanus points out all the rivers and streams that make up the world's waters. And guess what? They're his kids!

③ FIND AMPHITRITE

◀ As you zoom the curves, watch out for Amphitrite. This Nereid is hiding from Poseidon, but if you can spot her, you'll win a free ride!

④ SEE THE FUTURE WITH NEREUS ▼

If Nereus can't see what's ahead for you, nobody can! This proud papa of over 50 sea nymphs will be happy to tell you about the time he helped the mighty Heracles collect Hera's golden apples. Interested in shape-shifting? Nereus can help you transform into your wildest dream.

⑦ PHORCYS'S PETTING ZOO ▲

Phorcys knows beastly creatures (he's produced a few himself!). You'll appreciate his expertise as he leads you through his water-wildlife zoo. Pet a scaly serpent, ride a dragon, or swim with a sea monster! Caution: Please do not feed the animals. If they're hungry, you'll know it!

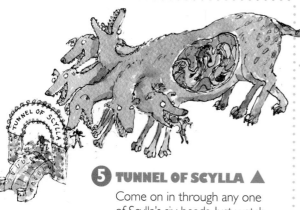

⑤ TUNNEL OF SCYLLA ▲

Come on in through any one of Scylla's six heads. Just watch out for her teeth as you go! And don't worry, you'll find your way out again … maybe.

◄⑧ GLAUCUS'S SEAWEED GARDEN

Enjoy the tranquility of Glaucus's garden. See the amazing immortal fish. Nibble on Glaucus's "magic plant," and experience immortality. Notice: Children under 18 must have a parent's permission to become immortal.

⑥ PONTUS'S WATER FLUME ▼

Ready for the wettest, wildest ride in the park? Splash over to the Water Flume, where Pontus, the original "Granddaddy of the Ocean and All the Fish in the Sea" awaits. Dive onto his mile-long waterbeard and experience what it's like to be part of the ocean.

⑨ PROTEUS'S FUN HOUSE OF MIRRORS ▼

Is that an animal, vegetable, or mineral? It's Proteus, the shape-shifting host of the House of Mirrors! Take a peek in his Mirror of the Future and get a glimpse of what you'll look like when you're his age!

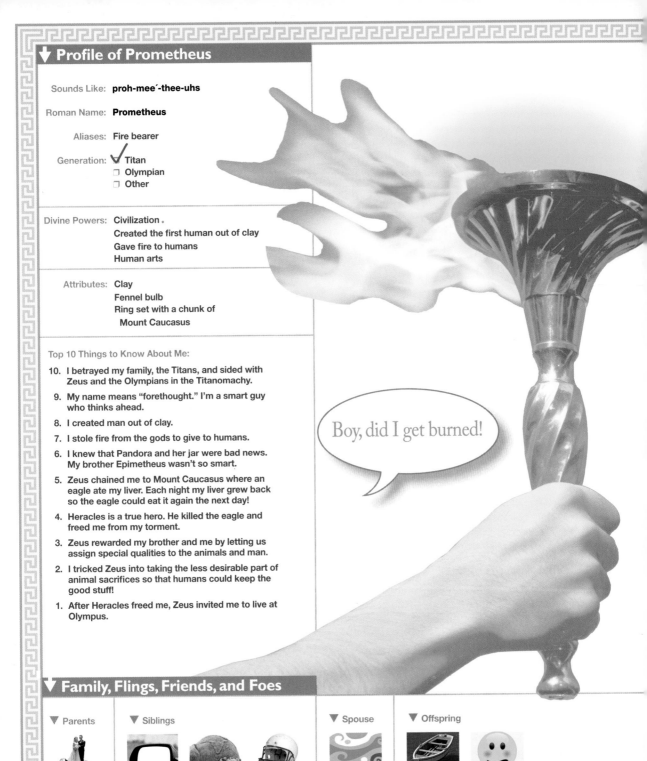

▼ Profile of Prometheus

Sounds Like: **proh-mee´-thee-uhs**

Roman Name: **Prometheus**

Aliases: Fire bearer

Generation: ✓ Titan
☐ Olympian
☐ Other

Divine Powers: Civilization .
Created the first human out of clay
Gave fire to humans
Human arts

Attributes: Clay
Fennel bulb
Ring set with a chunk of
Mount Caucasus

Top 10 Things to Know About Me:

10. I betrayed my family, the Titans, and sided with Zeus and the Olympians in the Titanomachy.

9. My name means "forethought." I'm a smart guy who thinks ahead.

8. I created man out of clay.

7. I stole fire from the gods to give to humans.

6. I knew that Pandora and her jar were bad news. My brother Epimetheus wasn't so smart.

5. Zeus chained me to Mount Caucasus where an eagle ate my liver. Each night my liver grew back so the eagle could eat it again the next day!

4. Heracles is a true hero. He killed the eagle and freed me from my torment.

3. Zeus rewarded my brother and me by letting us assign special qualities to the animals and man.

2. I tricked Zeus into taking the less desirable part of animal sacrifices so that humans could keep the good stuff!

1. After Heracles freed me, Zeus invited me to live at Olympus.

Boy, did I get burned!

▼ Family, Flings, Friends, and Foes

▼ Parents

Iapetus and Clymene

▼ Siblings

Epimetheus

Atlas

Menoetius

▼ Spouse

Asia

▼ Offspring

Deucalion

Aidos

PROMETHEUS

MAN'S BEST FRIEND

HELP! Somebody! Over here! I can't believe this. I've been chained to this mountain forever! Can anybody hear me? *Ahh! Ow!* At this very moment, an eagle is eating my liver. I MEAN, REALLY EATING MY LIVER!!!! *Ouch!* What did I do to deserve this? I made humans with my bare hands. BARE HANDS. Okay, so I took a little fire from Mount Olympus for my mortals. I mean, come *on*! Holy Zeus! Enough's enough, dude! *OW!*

REALITY CHECK

Humans have always worshipped fire. In fact, the idea of a ceremonial fire continues to this day. Each Olympic Games officially begins when a flame in the Olympic stadium is ignited by a blazing torch carried from Olympia, Greece, site of the first Olympic games.

Want to know more? Go to: http://www.greece.org/ olympics/flame/modern.html

I *hate* liver!

▼ Flings

Pandora **Hesione** **Pyrrha** **Pronoia**

▼ Friends

Heracles **Humankind**

▼ Foes

Zeus **Eagles** **Vultures**

Προμηθευς

PROMETHEUS

"I'm a people person!"

MYTHLOPEDIA

"These people are so cute, I think I'll make some more!"

IT'S GREEK TO ME

All cultures have creation stories that attempt to explain how the world and the things in it came to be. Some stories say that humans came out of an egg, or that they descended from the sky, or ascended from under the earth. Others have humans being born from the womb of Mother Earth or made from earth, clay, or stones.

"Prometheus Fountain" Rockefeller Center, NYC

MEET YOUR MAKER

Prometheus creates the first humans—out of clay!

Prometheus, a son of the Titan Iapetus and the sea **nymph** Clymene, supported Zeus in the epic battle for supremacy between the Olympians and the Titans. He became, for a time, a trusted adviser to Zeus. This smart and crafty god is credited with creating the first humans out of clay. Prometheus made **mortal** men only—no women. He soon found that his godly heart had a soft spot for these fascinating, flawed creatures. In fact, Prometheus became so fond of humans that he was willing to risk displeasing the powerful and vengeful Zeus— just to make life easier for the humans he had created.

Prometheus making people

OH, BROTHER!

Epimetheus is not quite as sharp as his brother Prometheus.

Prometheus, whose name signifies "forethought," never made a decision without considering its possible consequences. This ability helped him realize that Zeus would ultimately be victorious in the Titanomachy, the battle between the Olympians and Titans, and so he betrayed his Titan relatives to side with Zeus. He also convinced his brother Epimetheus to join him. Epimetheus's name signifies "afterthought." Unlike Prometheus, Epimetheus was always quick to act, never stopping to consider the consequences of his actions. After Zeus and the other Olympians defeated the Titans,

Zeus rewarded Prometheus and Epimetheus for their loyalty by allowing them to assign qualities to all the animals in the world. Foolish Epimetheus ran through the task so quickly—making a lion fierce and a hare swift—that he ran out of special traits, and there were none left for humans.

But Prometheus wasn't about to let his human creations go without, even if it meant that he would have to risk everything.

They showed their talents at an early age!

SACRIFICE SCANDAL

Prometheus makes an offering and it makes Zeus mad.

When **mortals** made sacrifices to the gods, Prometheus was there—watching out for humans! He took a sacrificed cow and cleverly divided it into two piles. One pile contained the choicest meats, which Prometheus covered with an unappetizing layer of bone, skin, and gristle. The other pile contained bones, fat, and gristle only, which Prometheus covered beneath the cow's fat so it looked desirable. He then offered Zeus his pick of the two piles. Zeus fell for the trick and picked the pile that looked the best, but contained the worst parts of the cow.

Zeus quickly realized that he'd been tricked by Prometheus—but since Zeus himself had picked the lesser offering, there was little he could do about it. From then on, sacrifices to the gods consisted of gristle, bones, and fat—while mortals got the meat.

> "Zeus, don't you want this delicious pile of cow sacrifice? Mmm!"

LIGHT MY FIRE

Prometheus risks everything to steal fire from the gods.

To get even with Prometheus for tricking the gods into choosing the inferior portion of the sacrificed cow, Zeus decided to deny fire to mortals. But Prometheus knew that fire would be a wonderful gift for humans—and he wasn't about to let the most powerful **deity** in the **pantheon** stand in his way. So Prometheus stole a single ember from the hearth at Mount Olympus and placed it in a hollowed-out **fennel** stalk for safekeeping. Prometheus made it down the mountain safely and presented fire to humans. With fire, humans became civilized: They made tools, built houses, and cooked food. Prometheus was right— fire was the perfect gift, after all!

Human portion

Gods' portion

Pandora

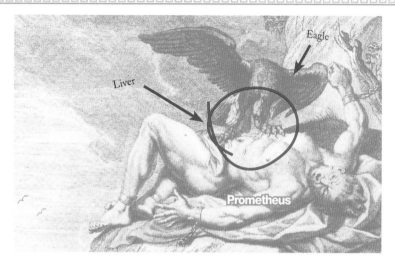

Eagle

Liver

Prometheus

THE GIFT THAT KEEPS ON GIVING

Pandora's jar holds trouble for all.

To punish Prometheus for stealing fire, Zeus decided to torment his prized creation—humans. So Zeus asked Hephaestus to craft the first woman, a **beguiling** creature named Pandora. Pandora, whose name means "all gifts," was endowed by the gods with beauty and charm. Then she was given a magic jar (often called a box) and told not to open it. Prometheus had warned his brother Epimetheus not to accept any gifts from Zeus. Still, he jumped at the chance to take Pandora for his bride. Together Epimetheus and Pandora gave in to their curiosity and opened the magic jar. Bad move! All the terrible evils of the world flew out, forever to torment humans. All that remained in the jar was hope.

FOR THE BIRDS

Zeus puts Prometheus in some serious time-out.

Zeus was furious that Prometheus had tricked the gods into taking the inferior offering of meat, then had given fire to humans. He couldn't allow anyone—not even a favored adviser like Prometheus—to disobey him so publicly and so often. As punishment, he had Prometheus chained to a boulder atop Mount Caucasus. There, a hungry eagle swooped down every day to peck at Prometheus's liver. By sundown, his liver was entirely consumed, but overnight it would grow back, and the eagle would return for another feast. Prometheus endured the agony because his gift of foresight had revealed to him that eventually he would be rescued from this torment. It took 13 generations but finally the hero Heracles was born, a child of Zeus and Alcmene. During a trial of his own, Heracles stumbled across Prometheus and freed him. Finally ready to forgive Prometheus, Zeus welcomed him to Olympus. Zeus presented Prometheus with a ring inset with a stone from Mount Caucasus so that he would never forget the punishment for his disobedience. As if he ever could!

REALITY CHECK

The ring that Zeus gave to Prometheus may have been the first ring in history! When humans wore rings after that, they did so to honor Prometheus, who was always so supportive of them.

▼ Profile of Uranus

Sounds Like:	**yur´-uh-nuhs**
Roman Name:	**Caelus**
Aliases:	**Sky**
Generation:	☐ **Titan**
	☐ **Olympian**
	☑ **Other**
Divine Powers:	**Personification of the sky**
	Sky and heavens
Attributes:	**Cape covered with stars**

I can't get no respect!

Top 10 Things to Know About Me:

10. I predicted the downfall of the Titans in their battle with the Olympians.

9. Gaea, the earth, created me, and then we got together.

8. I was so terrified of my first kids—the giant one-eyed Cyclopes and the hundred-handed Hecatoncheires—that I sent them to Tartarus for a time-out.

7. Gaea convinced my own kids to attack me!

6. My son Cronus took my place as ruler of everything—until Zeus attacked him.

5. The ancient Greeks envisioned the sky as a solid brass, star-covered dome that arched over the earth.

4. Zeus forced Atlas to hold me up, up, up and away from the earth.

3. The seventh planet in the solar system is named for me.

2. Would you like to see a picture of my grandson Zeus?

1. Cronus's attack on me led to the creation of the Furies and Aphrodite.

▼ Family, Flings, Friends, and Foes

▼ Parent	▼ Spouse	▼ Offspring						
Gaea	Gaea	The Titans	The Hecatoncheires	Oceanus	Aphrodite	The Furies	The Gigantes	The Cyclopes

URANUS
I WAS HERE FIRST!

Listen, you whippersnappers—it's time you paid respect to the original god of the gods! You think you're hot stuff, but you wouldn't be here without *me*! Back in my day, I was the best of them all. You don't get bigger than the sky. Your grandmother and I populated this whole universe. Can you blame me for not wanting you to be born? Look how you've treated me! Show a little respect to an old god. And keep it down out there!

Chill out, old man.

▼ Friends

Atlas

▼ Foes

His Offspring

Cyclops

URANUS

"Stick with me and I'll make you a star!"

MYTHLOPEDIA

Ουρανος

IT'S GREEK TO ME

In Greek mythology, Uranus is the personification of the sky, and there are two explanations for how the sky is held up. One story claims that as punishment for siding with the Titans in their war against the Olympians, Zeus forced Atlas to hold up the sky. In another story, the sky was held above the earth on four pillars. In fact, some versions of the story say the pillars are Uranus's sons.

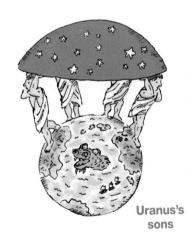

Uranus's sons

TITANS TRAPPED IN TARTARUS

Paranoid Uranus locks up his own offspring.

Uranus and Gaea were the parents of all 12 Titans, as well as the hundred-handed giants known as the Hecatoncheires, and the one-eyed giants, the Cyclopes. Uranus was both terrified and disgusted by his offsprings' monstrous appearances and their tremendous strength. Afraid that his powerful children would one day overthrow him, he refused to allow any of them to be born. Instead he imprisoned them in Tartarus, deep inside Gaea. This caused Gaea such agonizing pain that she grew to hate Uranus. She conspired with her Titan sons to overthrow Uranus, and provided Cronus with a sharp sickle, or curved knife, for the job. One night, when Uranus least expected it, Cronus attacked him with the sickle. The Titans were then free and Cronus replaced Uranus as the most powerful **deity**. Uranus's worst fear had come true—and largely because of his own actions.

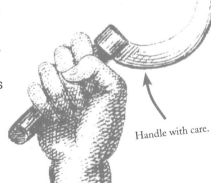

Handle with care.

DADDY'S LITTLE MONSTERS

Uranus thinks his kids are a giant mistake!

Uranus hated his offspring, particularly the giants he had fathered, the Hecatoncheires and the Cyclopes. The Hecatoncheires—Cottus, Briareus, and Gyes—each had 50 heads and 100 hands. These fierce and brutal beings were responsible for causing terrible storms and hurricanes.

The Cyclopes, named Brontes, Steropes, and Arges, were massive, one-eyed giants.

Uranus dealt with his fear of these creatures by imprisoning them with the Titans in Tartarus, the deepest part of the **Underworld**. After Cronus overthrew Uranus, he kept the Hecatoncheires and Cyclopes imprisoned. This came in handy for Zeus, who later freed them in exchange for their support during the Titanomachy, a war between the Titans and Oympians. The Cyclopes made the weapons that helped Zeus win the war: his thunderbolt, Poseidon's **trident**, and Hades' helmet of invisibility.

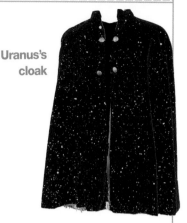

Uranus's cloak

SKY'S THE LIMIT

Uranus is also the personification of the sky.

In addition to being the first god of the sky and heavens, Uranus was also a **personification** of the sky. He wore a cloak that was covered with stars; at night he would come down to cover the earth (Gaea) and mate with her. Later, after Cronus overthrew him and Uranus lost power, he was simply the sky, envisioned as a star-spangled bronze dome that arched over the earth, held high by Atlas.

Uranus

"You gods today don't know the meaning of work."

99

▼ Profile of Wind Gods

Sounds Like: **bor´-ee-uhs; zef´-uh-rus; noh´-tus; yur´-us**

Roman Names: **Aquilo (Boreas), Favonius (Zephyrus), Auster (Notus), Vulturnus (Eurus)**

Generation: ☐ **Titan**
☐ **Olympian**
☑ **Other**

Divine Powers: **Personifications of winds**

Attributes: **Boreas: Clouds, Conch shell, Long beard, Purple wings, Warm cloak**

Zephyrus: Flowers, Fruits, Warm winds

Eurus and Notus: Capes

Top 10 Things to Know About Us:

10. Boreas here. With my frosty breath, I blow the cold winds that bring winter to Greece.

9. I kidnapped and married Princess Orithyia of Athens, so the Athenians consider me family.

8. I helped the Athenians by sinking four hundred Persian ships!

7. The Hyperboreans live in a mystical land that has endless warm weather since I never visit. And they're always happy!

6. I have purple wings and look like an old man with a long, white beard. It's a fashion statement.

5. It's me, Zephyrus. I have wings, too, but I'm young and handsome.

4. With my warm breath, I bring spring to Greece.

3. Here's the sad part: I accidentally killed Hyacinthus in a jealous rage.

2. I'm the father of Achilles' talking horses, Balius and Xanthus.

1. My wife Chloris is the goddess of flowers, and our son Carpus is the god of fruit.

▼ Family, Flings, Friends, and Foes

▼ Parents	▼ Siblings		▼ Spouses			▼ Offspring (Boreas)	
Astraeus and Eos	**Iris**	**Chloris**	**Boreas: Orithyia**	**Zephyrus: Chloris**	**Iris**	**Khione**	**The Boreades**

WIND GODS

WILD WINDS

Time for your local "Weather Update" with your favorite wind god, Zephyrus! Here's the scoop on what my brothers are up to today. Boreas, the cold north wind, is making his way down from that miserable cave he lives in. Brrr! Bundle up, because Notus isn't blowing searing southern winds today. Leave your umbrella at home, since there's no chance of warm, wet weather with east wind Eurus out of the picture. But don't worry, I'll be blowing warm spring winds before you know it!

▼ Offspring (Zephyrus)

Carpus   **Aellopos**   **Balius and Xanthus**

▼ Flings (Zephyrus)

Hyacinthus

▼ Friends

The Athenians

▼ Foes

Boreas: Xerxes   **Zephyrus: Apollo**

"We're blowing your way!"

MYTI LOPEDI

WIND GODS

IT'S GREEK TO ME

According to Greek mythology, the god Zeus made King Aeolus the ruler of the winds. Aeolus kept the winds in caves on an island in his kingdom. He would release them when the gods ordered him to do so, or simply when he wished to. Depending on which wind he released, the result could range from a pleasant breeze to a violent storm.

BOREAS

The wintry North Wind sends a chill.

Boreas was the strongest of all the winds. Often pictured as an old man with a white beard and purple wings, Boreas tried to win the heart of the Athenian princess Orithyia. When he wasn't successful, he took action another way: He simply carried the princess off in a great gust of wind.

Because of his relationship with Orithyia, the Athenians thought of Boreas as one of their own. So they asked for his help defending themselves against the Persian navy. He caused a violent storm, and four hundred Persian ships were destroyed. After that, Boreas was worshipped in Athens and a festival was named for him.

Boreas and Orithyia later had two winged sons, Calais and Zetes, known as the Boreades, who traveled with the heroes Jason and the Argonauts in the quest for the Golden Fleece. The Argonauts sent the Boreades to chase away the monstrous Harpies, who tormented Phineus, a blind seer. In exchange for the Boreades saving the day for Phineus, the seer agreed to help the Argonauts find the Golden Fleece.

REALITY CHECK

The Boreas Pass Route running from Como to Breckenridge, Colorado, was named for the North Wind.

ZEPHYRUS

The gentle West Wind brings spring breezes.

Usually pictured as handsome winged youth carrying flowers in a fold of his cloak, Zephyrus was the gentlest and most welcome of all winds. He and his wife, Chloris, goddess of flowers and fruits, were the parents of Carpus, the god of fruits (like his mom).

He was also the father of the immortal talking horses Balius and Xanthus. These two horses could run like the wind—and no wonder! Not only was their father a wind, but so was their mother. She was the hideous Harpy Podarge, a stormy wind. Poseidon, god of the sea, gave Balius and Xanthus as a wedding gift to Peleus and Thetis, a sea **nymph**. Peleus later gave these horses to his son Achilles, who used them to pull his **chariot** in the Trojan War.

NOTUS AND EURUS

Warm winds blow from two directions.

Boreas and Zephyrus had two brothers who were also wind gods. Notus was the god of the warm south wind and he brought rain and fog when he blew. Eurus was the god of the east wind and his breath caused rain and melted the snows.

Along with Boreas, these two gods brought trouble for the hero Odysseus. When Odysseus and his crew were on their way home from the Trojan War, they landed on an island that was ruled by King Aeolus, who was also ruler of the winds. Aeolus welcomed them and gave Odysseus a gift: Boreas, Notus, and Eurus all tied up in a bag. Zephyrus was not in the bag; his job was to help by gently blowing Odysseus's ship home. When they were nearly home, the crew became curious about what was in the bag. One sailor opened it while Odysseus slept. The three winds rushed out and blew the ship right back to Aeolus's kingdom. This time, Aeolus was not so generous and the crew had to continue without any help from the winds.

Notus

Eurus

He's full of hot air!

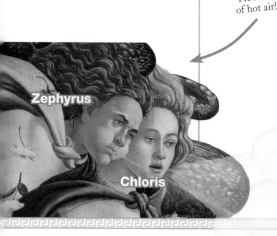

Zephyrus

Chloris

Thanks, dude!

▼ Profile of Zeus

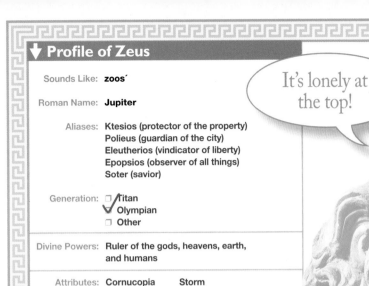

> It's lonely at the top!

Sounds Like: **zoos´**

Roman Name: **Jupiter**

Aliases: Ktesios (protector of the property)
Polieus (guardian of the city)
Eleutherios (vindicator of liberty)
Epopsios (observer of all things)
Soter (savior)

Generation: ☐ Titan
☑ Olympian
☐ Other

Divine Powers: Ruler of the gods, heavens, earth, and humans

Attributes:
Cornucopia	Storm
Eagle	Thunderbolt
Mountaintop	Wreath of oak or
Oak	olive leaves
Scepter	Weather
Shield	

Top 10 Things to Know About Me:

10. I had over 115 girlfriends and wives—and over 140 children!

9. I saved my brothers and sisters from our dad, Cronus, who had swallowed each one!

8. My mom saved me from my dad by hiding me in a cave, where nymphs secretly raised me on the milk of a sacred goat, Amaltheia.

7. My jealous wife, Hera, always wanted to get even with my girlfriends.

6. The Cyclopes made special thunderbolts that I threw to punish anyone who disobeyed me.

5. My daughter, the goddess Athena, burst out of my head fully formed!

4. I spent ten years leading the Olympians in a battle with the Titans—and won!

3. I invented some terrible punishments—just ask Prometheus!

2. As a weather god, I control the amount of rain that falls.

1. I became ruler of the gods, the heavens, and mortals by drawing lots with my brothers, Poseidon and Hades.

▼ Family, Flings, Friends, and Foes

▼ Parents

Cronus and Rhea

▼ Siblings

Poseidon

Hades

Demeter

Hera

Hestia

▼ Spouse

Hera

▼ Offspring

Ares

Athena

ZEUS
BIG DADDY

Kids! Settle down! Do you want to go back to Olympus? Because we will. I will turn this chariot around *right now*. I see everything, remember? Don't make me hurl my thunderbolts. Stop squabbling—you're *all* important gods, okay? You're giving me a splitting headache. With 140 kids, I don't have time to deal with your problems. There's a world of human problems I have to solve, too! I know it's not fair.

Just be glad I didn't swallow you when you were born!

REALITY CHECK
In the video game *Master of Olympus: Zeus*, players build a city in ancient Greece. The Olympians—including Zeus—can bless or curse the city.

Hera

I'll show you lonely, Mr. Two-Timer!

Apollo

▼ Flings

Leto

Semele

▼ Friends

Tiresias

Gaea

The Cyclopes

▼ Foes

Tantalus

Sisyphus

Cronus

Ζευς

IT'S GREEK TO ME

As the supreme ruler on Mount Olympus, Zeus had many jobs. He was the ruler of the weather and produced rain and storms. He was also the keeper of laws and responsible for making sure that both gods and **mortals** followed them. He was the protector of Greek kings and their families, the guardian of morality, and the source of prophecies. Quite the busy god!

This stuff will really do a number on you!

vomit potion

COUGH IT UP, CRONUS!

Rhea puts one over on Cronus.

After the Titan Cronus overthrew his father, Uranus, and freed his Titan siblings from Tartarus, he started a family of his own with his wife and sister, Rhea. But when Cronus heard a **prophecy** that he would be overthrown by his own son, he became as paranoid and fearful as Uranus had been. Cronus decided that the only way he could prevent the prophecy from coming true would be to swallow his children whole as each one was born! And so Poseidon, Hades, Demeter, Hestia, and Hera were all swallowed.

Rhea soon grew tired of losing her children this way. She hatched a plan with her mother-in-law, Gaea. When Rhea's sixth child, Zeus, was born, she was ready to trick Cronus.

Rhea presented Cronus with a stone wrapped in blankets, which he promptly swallowed without even looking at it. Then Rhea hid baby Zeus on the island of Crete, where he was raised by **nymphs**.

Cronus never suspected that one of his children had escaped. When Zeus reached adulthood, he disguised himself as Cronus's **cupbearer** and snuck a **potion** into Cronus's drink that made him vomit up all of Zeus's siblings. Zeus was finally joined by his powerful siblings, and they were ready to begin a war against the father who had tried to oppress them.

TRIUMPH IN THE TITANOMACHY

Zeus plays to win—and he wins it all in the war with the Titans.

Zeus knew that he and the Olympians would never be safe while Cronus was in power. So once his siblings had become free, Zeus started a war with the Titans called the Titanomachy. The war raged for ten years. It involved a great number of powerful creatures, gods, and goddesses. Led by Cronus, the powerful Titans fought on one side. On the other side, Zeus was joined by his siblings Poseidon, Hades, Demeter, Hera, and Hestia. The Titans Prometheus and Epimetheus betrayed their family by joining with Zeus.

The turning point of the war came when Zeus freed the Hecatoncheires and the Cyclopes from Tartarus in exchange for their loyalty during the war. With their strength on his side, Zeus was bound to win—especially when the Cyclopes

Thunderbolt

Helmet of Invisibility

Trident

Weapons Courtesy of the Cyclopes

created three powerful weapons for the Olympians: Zeus's thunderbolts, Poseidon's trident, and Hades' helmet of invisibility. When the Titans finally surrendered, Zeus imprisoned them in Tartarus so that they would not be a threat anymore—and the era of the Olympians officially began.

THE FIRST OLYMPICS

Let the games begin—as long as they honor Zeus!

Some stories claim that the Olympics were founded by the hero Heracles, Zeus's son with Alcmene. According to these stories, Heracles started the games to honor Zeus. But according to other stories, a ferocious wrestling match between Zeus and Cronus marked the first Olympic Games. Still other stories say that Zeus instituted the Olympic Games as a tradition to mark his victory in the Titanomachy.

REALITY CHECK

Historical record shows that the Olympic Games were officially founded in 776 BCE in Olympia, Greece. The first 13 Olympics featured just one event: a foot race. Over the years more events were added, including wrestling, boxing, chariot races, and armored fighting.

We're with you, Zeus.

The Cyclopes

First Olympics

DADDY OF THEM ALL

Zeus is in the house.

Of all his amazing powers and accomplishments, Zeus may be best known for his numerous love affairs—and his huge family! As the most powerful god in the **pantheon**, when Zeus desired someone— **mortal**, god, or goddess—nothing could stand in his way, much to the dismay of his wife, Hera. Zeus had relationships with more than 115 females, starting with his first wife, Metis, whom he swallowed when it was prophesied that she would bear a child more powerful than Zeus.

Next Zeus married his sister, Hera, in a match that caused her great unhappiness. Hera was consumed by jealousy whenever she thought of Zeus's other

"We're all one big, happy family!"

loves, and she was determined to make their lives miserable. Zeus's girlfriends, especially Callisto, Io, Semele, and Leto, all suffered under Hera's attentions. Despite the grief his wandering eye caused Hera, Zeus continued in his ways, fathering some of the most powerful gods, goddesses, and mortals, including Apollo, Artemis, Athena, Dionysus, Hermes, Heracles, Helen of Troy, Perseus, Tantalus, Orion, and Minos. With Hera, Zeus's children included Ares, Hebe, and Eileithyia.

Let's play catch!

MO

From the Desk of **ZEUS**

To: All major and minor deities

It has come to my attention that my wife, Hera, may be intimidating some of you, especially those of you who are charming and attractive. Fear not, for Hera will be severely punished if she continues this behavior. None of you should be afraid of getting to know me better … say, in my palace, over a gourmet, candlelight dinner of nectar and ambrosia. Just tell me when, and I'll make all the arrangements!

Z

ATTENDANTS ON OLYMPUS

Even Zeus needs a little advice sometimes.

Zeus was almighty, but that didn't mean he wanted to do everything himself! So he wisely surrounded himself with trusted advisers: the goddesses Themis, Dike, Nemesis, and Nike. Themis was a Titan and the guardian of divine law and order. She gave good advice to Zeus—and he liked it so much that he made her his girlfriend!

Themis and Zeus had a daughter, Dike, who was the goddess of human justice. Dike advised Zeus about the problems of mortals. Nemesis, the goddess of **retribution**, may also have been a daughter of Zeus. She handed out fortune and misfortune to humans, making sure that all mortals had their share of sadness and tragedy. Nike, the goddess of victory, was another ally of Zeus's—a smart move on his part, given the battles he engaged in (like the Titanomachy) and some of the power plays that took place on Mount Olympus.

DANAË AND PERSEUS

Zeus helps a prophecy come true—and has another kid, too!

Danaë was the daughter of King Acrisius of Argos, who imprisoned her because of a **prophecy** that her son would kill him. Zeus fell in love with Danaë. Because she was locked away, Zeus transformed himself into a shower of gold and poured into her chamber. Danaë later gave birth to Zeus's son Perseus.

King Acrisius was not willing to give in to the prophecy yet. He locked Danaë and Perseus in a large chest and set them adrift in the sea, where they floated aimlessly. Zeus intervened, guiding the chest to the shores of the island of Seriphos, where King Polydectes welcomed them. Polydectes soon fell in love with Danaë and tried to get rid of Perseus by setting him on an impossible task: slaying the monstrous Gorgon Medusa.

Perseus proved himself a hero when he killed Medusa and then used her **severed** head to turn Polydectes to stone so he could rescue his mother. Acrisius tried to flee from his grandson Perseus, but the prophecy was fulfilled when Perseus accidentally killed his grandfather during a discus-throwing competition.

Zeus sneaks in through the ceiling.

FAMILY TREE

KEY

 = LOVERS

 = MARRIED

- - - - - = RELATIONSHIP

- - - - - = ZEUS'S RELATIONSHIPs

———— = OFFSPRING

CAPS = OLYMPIAN

 = TITAN

 = MALE

 = FEMALE

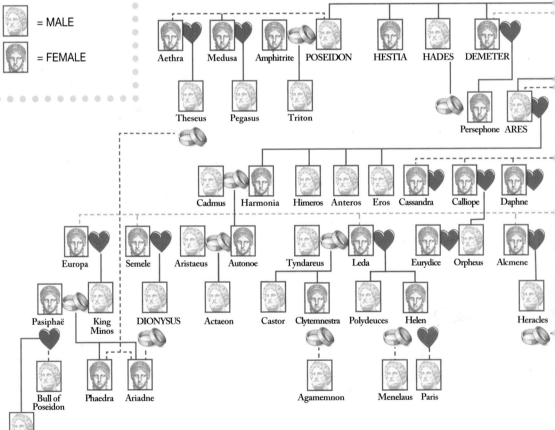

Aethra Medusa Amphitrite POSEIDON HESTIA HADES DEMETER

Theseus Pegasus Triton

Persephone ARES

Cadmus Harmonia Himeros Anteros Eros Cassandra Calliope Daphne

Europa Semele Aristaeus Autonoe Tyndareus Leda Eurydice Orpheus Alcmene

Pasiphaë King Minos DIONYSUS Actaeon Castor Clytemnestra Polydeuces Helen Heracles

Bull of Poseidon Phaedra Ariadne Agamemnon Menelaus Paris

Minotaur

114

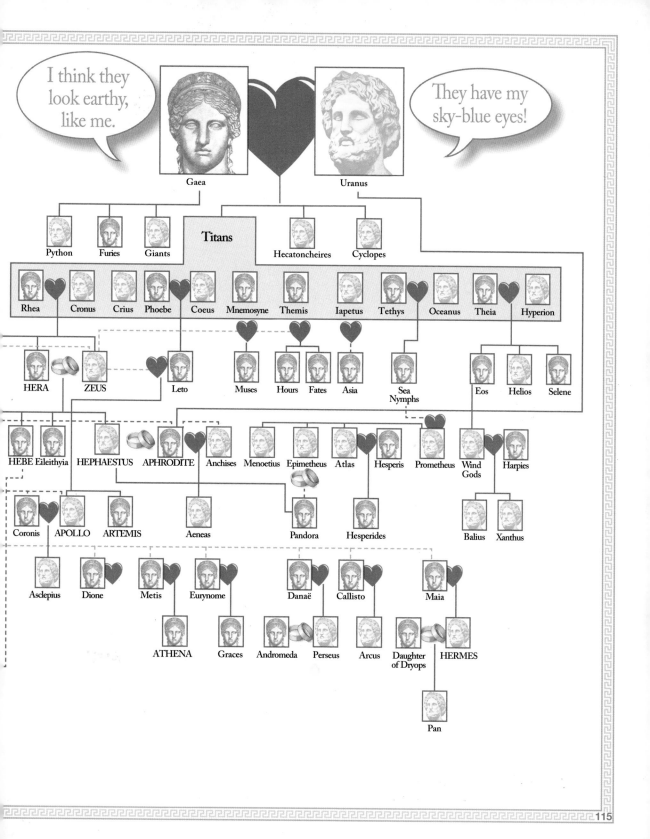

GLOSSARY

ambrosia   the food of the gods

Asclepieion   a healing temple sacred to the god Asclepius

aureole   a radiant circle of light that surrounds the head of a god; halo

beguiling   charming

caduceus   a staff with two snakes twined around it and two wings at its top

careened   lurched, or swayed abruptly

Centaur   a creature with the head and upper body of a human and the legs and lower body of a horse

Chaos   a vast, empty state of nothingness that existed before the earth came into being

chariot   a two-wheeled vehicle drawn by horses

chasm   a deep, gaping crack in the earth

cupbearer   one whose job it is to fill wine cups and serve them

deity   a god or goddess

Dionysia   a festival held to honor the god Dionysus

fennel   a plant from the parsley family, with small yellow flowers

herald   one who delivers messages or announces something to come

isthmus   a narrow strip of land bordered by water and connecting two larger areas of land

lots   a group of objects (often shards of pottery) used to make a choice by chance

lyre   a U-shaped stringed instrument related to the harp

maze   a complicated, confusing arrangement of paths

mortal   a human being; also, subject to death

nectar   the drink of the gods

nymph   a female spirit associated with nature

omphalos   a central point; in Apollo's temple, a stone believed to mark the earth's center

oracle   a priestess or priest who communicated the response of a god to a questioner and the response itself; also, the god's shrine

panpipe	a wind instrument made from a set of reeds of different lengths, tied together
pantheon	all the gods of a particular group of people
patron	a special guardian or supporter
personification	giving human qualities to nonhuman objects or ideas
potion	a mixture of liquids given as medicine or for magical reasons
prophecy	a prediction of a future event
prophet	one who foretells the future, often inspired by the gods
pyre	a woodpile used for burning a body as part of a funeral rite
retribution	something given in payment, usually as a punishment
satyr	a mythological creature that is part human, part horse or goat

severed	removed by cutting off or breaking apart
transfigure	to transform in appearance
trident	a spear with three prongs
tripod	a three-legged support, often used to hold a cauldron for cooking over a fire
Underworld	in Greek mythology, the world of the dead, ruled by the god Hades
urn	a container usually with a base or pedestal
venomous	poisonous
vial	a small container that can be closed, often used to hold liquids

PEGASUS
Zeus placed the winged horse among the stars. Only the front half of his body is shown.

ANDROMEDA
Andromeda was chained to a rock in the sea, threatened by a sea monster, and rescued by the hero Perseus.

CYGNUS
Cygnus the Swan is also known as the Northern Cross. Some mythographers claim the swan is Zeus in disguise.

LYRA
The lyre of the great musician Orpheus was placed among the stars by the Muses.

PERSEUS
The hero slayed the monster Medusa and rescued Andromeda, from Cetus, a sea monster. He is shown holding Medusa's head.

HERACLES
Shown kneeling, holding a club, the great hero Heracles was turned into a constellation by Zeus.

Northern Hemisphere

URSA MAJOR
(Great Bear)
Callisto was turned into a bear and shot by Artemis. Zeus placed her among the stars, where she keeps an eye out for Orion, the hunter.

LEO
(Nemean Lion)
The lion of Nemea was slain by the hero Heracles as one of his twelve labors.

ORION

The famed hunter Orion boasted that he would kill every animal on Earth, so Gaea sent a scorpion to sting him. Zeus placed the hunter among the stars and the scorpion nearby *(continues from the Northern Hemisphere to the Southern Hemisphere)*.

CETUS

This sea monster was sent by Poseidon to punish Cassiopeia, the mother of Andromeda, for her vanity.

STARS
OF GREEK
MYTHOLOGY

Many constellations were named for characters in classical mythology. The practice of taking a being or an object and placing it among the stars is called *catasterism*.

SCORPIO

Sent by Gaea to sting the hunter Orion, the scorpion is placed near him in the sky to remind him of the consequences of boasting.

CENTAURUS

Centaurus represents the wise Centaur Chiron. Its brightest star, Alpha Centauri, is the closest star to the sun.

Southern Hemisphere

ARGO

The ancient constellation Argo Navis, named for the ship that carried Jason and the Argonauts, is made up of three smaller constellations: Puppis (the stern), Carina (the keel), and Vela (the sails).

HYDRA

The serpent was killed by Heracles as another of his twelve labors. In the sky, Hydra is the largest of the 88 constellations *(continues from the Northern Hemisphere to the Southern Hemisphere)*.

119

note on page 128

FURTHER READING

Bolton, Lesley. *The Everything Classical Mythology Book*. Avon, MA: Adams Media, 2002.

Bulfinch, Thomas. *Bulfinch's Greek and Roman Mythology: The Age of Fable.* Mineola, NY: Dover Publications, 2000.

D'Aulaire, Ingri, and Edgar Parin D'Aulaire. *D'Aulaire's Book of Greek Myths.* New York: Random House, Delacorte Press, 1992.

Fleischman, Paul. *Dateline: Troy*. Cambridge, MA: Candlewick Press, 2006.

Hansen, William. *Classical Mythology: A Guide to the Mythical World of the Greeks and Romans*. New York: Oxford University Press, 2005.

Homer. *The Iliad*. Edited by E.V. Rieu. New York: Penguin Classics, 2003.

Homer. *The Odyssey.* Edited by Bernard Knox. New York: Penguin Classics, 2006.

Osborn, Kevin, and Dana L. Burgess. *The Complete Idiot's Guide to Classical Mythology*. 2nd ed. New York: Penguin, Alpha Books, 2004.

Roberts, Jennifer T., and Tracy Barrett. *The Ancient Greek World*. New York: Oxford University Press, 2004.

Sutcliff, Rosemary. *The Wanderings of Odysseus: The Story of the Odyssey*. New York: Random House, Laurel Leaf, 2005.

———. *Black Ships Before Troy*. London: Frances Lincoln, 2008.

WEB SITES

Encyclopedia Mythica: *http://pantheon.org/*
An online encyclopedia of mythology, folklore, and religion

Greek Mythology: *http://www.greekmythology.com/*
Contains information on gods, goddesses, beasts, and heroes as well as full text of selected books on Greek mythology and literature

Kidipede: Greek Myths: *http://www.historyforkids.org/learn/greeks/religion/greekrelig.htm*
Greek mythology pages of an online encyclopedia of history and science for middle-school students

Mythweb: *http://www.mythweb.com/*
An overview of the Olympians and selected heroes; includes teaching tips

Theoi Greek Mythology: *http://theoi.com/*
Profiles of the Greek gods and goddesses, and other characters from Greek mythology with an emphasis on their appearances in art and literature

INDEX

Marie O'Neill, Creative Director
Cheryl Clark, Editor in Chief
Caroline Anderson, Director of Photography
Cian O'Day, Ed Kasche, Jay Pastorello, Photo Research
SimonSays Design!, Book production and design

Illustrations:
Kevin Brimmer: 93, 110–111
Paul Meisel: Cover, 4–5, 6, 19, 28, 38–41, 56–57, 58, 59, 67, 69, 95, 98, 107,
108, 112–113,118–119, 121
Raphael Montoliu: 92
Rupert Van Wyk (Beehive Illustration): 7, 51, 86–87, 88, 89, 117
XNR Productions, Inc.: 118–119

Note: Constellations in illustration on pages 118–119 are not exactly where they appear
in the sky. For more accurate charts go to: www.astronomy.com